AMERICA'S BEST

Healthy

EATING

Table of Contents

Healthy Eating

Chicken Recipes

Fish & Seafood

Pasta Recipes

Low Calorie Recipes

Desserts

Tomato and Pepper Ice, a refreshing appetizer.

AMERICA'S BEST

Healthy

E A T I N G

Gazpacho

SERVES 4

Gazpacho is a typically Spanish soup which is served well chilled, accompanied by a selection of fresh vegetables.

PREPARATION: 20 mins, plus chilling

1 pound ripe tomatoes
1 onion, chopped
1 green pepper, diced
½ cucumber, chopped
2 tbsps day-old white breadcrumbs
2 cloves garlic, crushed
2 tbsps red wine vinegar
2½ cups tomato juice
Salt and freshly ground black pepper

Accompaniments
½ cucumber, diced
10 green onions (scallions), chopped
2 cups tomatoes, skinned, seeded and
    chopped
1 large green bell pepper, diced

1. Cut a small cross in the top of each of the tomatoes, and plunge into a bowl of boiling water for a few seconds.

2. Carefully peel the skin away from the blanched tomatoes. Discard the skin and chop the tomatoes coarsely, removing the tough cores.

Step 2
Carefully peel the skin away from the blanched tomatoes using a sharp knife.

3. Put the roughly-chopped tomatoes into a liquidizer or food processor, along with the onion, pepper, and cucumber. Blend until finely chopped.

4. Put the chopped vegetables into a bowl with the breadcrumbs, garlic, vinegar, and tomato juice. Mix well to blend evenly and allow to stand 15 minutes.

5. Season the soup thoroughly, then push through a fine-meshed sieve, using the back of a wooden spoon and working well to press all the vegetables through, but keeping the seeds out of the resulting purée.

6. Chill the soup well before serving, surrounded by bowls containing the accompaniments.

Mediterranean Eggplant

SERVES 2-4

These delicious stuffed eggplants can be served as an accompaniment to a main meal for four or as a lunch dish for two.

PREPARATION: 25 mins
COOKING: 40 mins

---

2 small eggplants
2 tbsps polyunsaturated margarine
1 small onion, finely chopped
1 clove garlic, crushed
2 tomatoes, skinned
⅔ cup long-grain rice, cooked
2 tsps fresh marjoram, chopped
Pinch of cinnamon
Salt and freshly ground black pepper

---

1. Wrap the eggplants in foil and bake in an oven preheated to 350°F for 20 minutes or until softened. Allow to cool.

2. Cut the eggplants in half lengthwise then using a serrated teaspoon or grapefruit knife, carefully scoop out the pulp leaving a ½-inch border to form a shell.

3. Melt the margarine in a skillet and gently sauté the onion and garlic until they are just soft.

4. Chop the eggplant pulp roughly and stir into the skillet along with the onions. Cover and cook about 5 minutes.

Step 2
Carefully scoop the pulp out of each eggplant half with a serrated spoon or grapefruit knife.

5. Quarter the tomatoes and remove and discard the seeds. Chop the tomato flesh roughly and stir into the cooked eggplant and onion mixture, along with the cooked rice, marjoram, and cinnamon. Season with salt and pepper.

6. Carefully pile the rice filling into the eggplant shells and arrange them in an ovenproof dish or on a baking tray. Cover with foil.

7. Return to the oven and bake 20 minutes. Serve hot, garnished with a little finely chopped parsley if wished.

Tomato and Pepper Ice

SERVES 4-6

Similar to frozen gazpacho, this appetizer is ideal for serving on warm summer days.

PREPARATION: 15 mins plus 2 hrs freezing

---

6 ice cubes
½ cup canned tomato juice
Juice of 1 lemon
1 tsp Worcestershire sauce
½ small green pepper, very finely chopped
½ small red pepper, very finely chopped

---

1. Put the ice into a thick plastic bag and break into small pieces using a rolling pin or steak hammer.

2. Put the broken ice into a blender or food processor, along with the tomato juice, lemon juice, and Worcestershire sauce. Blend the mixture until it becomes slushy.

Step 2 Blend the ice, tomato juice, lemon juice, and Worcestershire sauce until it becomes a smooth slush.

Step 5 During the freezing time, keep stirring the tomato and pepper ice with a fork.

3. Pour the tomato mixture into ice trays and freeze 30 minutes, or until it is just half-frozen.

4. Remove the tomato ice from the freezer trays and put it into a bowl. Mash the tomato ice with the back of a fork until the crystals are well broken up.

5. Mix in the chopped peppers and return the tomato ice to the freezer trays. Re-freeze for a further 1½ hours, stirring occasionally to prevent the mixture from solidifying completely.

6. To serve, allow the tomato ice to defrost about 5 minutes, then mash with the back of a fork to roughly break up the ice crystals. Serve in small chilled glass dishes or in tomato shells.

Zucchini, Caper, and Anchovy Salad

SERVES 4

The secret of this salad is to slice the raw zucchini really thinly.

PREPARATION: 15-20 mins

1 pound zucchini
1 small onion, thinly sliced
1 tbsp capers
4-6 canned anchovy fillets, chopped
1 tbsp anchovy oil (drained from the can of
    anchovy fillets)
2 tbsps olive oil
2 tbsps tarragon vinegar
Juice of ½ lemon
Salt and freshly ground black pepper to taste

1. Top and tail the zucchini, and slice them very thinly with a sharp knife, food processor, or mandolin.

2. Mix the sliced zucchini with the onion, capers and chopped anchovy fillets.

3. Mix the anchovy oil, olive oil, tarragon vinegar, and lemon juice together; add salt and pepper to taste.

4. Stir the dressing into the prepared salad ingredients.

Salade Paysanne

SERVES 6

This salad can be made with any selection of fresh vegetables, so whether it's winter or summer, there's no excuse for not serving a delicious fresh salad.

PREPARATION: 20 mins

4 green onions (scallions)
½ cucumber
3 carrots
6 large tomatoes, skinned
10 button mushrooms
3 sticks celery
1 green pepper, chopped
15-20 tiny cauliflower flowerets
15-20 baby radishes, quartered
1 tbsp chopped watercress, cress, or chia
2 sprigs fresh coriander (cilantro), or parsley, chopped
8 lettuce leaves for garnish

Dressing
½ tsp salt
½ tsp freshly ground black pepper
2 tbsps cider or wine vinegar
1 tbsp lemon juice
4 tbsps olive or vegetable oil
Pinch powdered mustard
Liquid sweetener to taste

1. Trim the green onions and slice them diagonally into thin slices.

2. Peel the cucumber and quarter it lengthwise. Use a sharp knife to remove the

Step 6 Whisk all the dressing ingredients together using a fork or balloon whisk, until the mixture becomes thick and cloudy.

soft, seedy center, discard this, and dice the remaining flesh.

3. Peel the carrots and slice them thinly, cutting the carrots diagonally with a sharp knife.

4. Quarter the skinned tomatoes and cut away the tough green cores.

5. Thinly slice the mushrooms and celery. Cut the pepper in half lengthwise, discard the seeds and stringy parts then chop the flesh.

6. Mix together all the dressing ingredients. Whisk thoroughly using a fork, or balloon whisk, until the mixture becomes thick and cloudy.

7. Arrange the lettuce leaves on a serving dish. Mix all the prepared vegetables together, and pile on top.

8. Just before serving, spoon a little of the dressing over the salad and serve the remainder separately in a small jug.

Vegetable and Olive Casserole

SERVES 6

The addition of vinegar and capers gives this refreshing vegetable dish a sharp twist to its flavor.

PREPARATION: 30 mins plus standing time
COOKING: 25 mins

---

1 eggplant
Salt
⅔ cup olive or sunflower oil
1 onion, thinly sliced
2 red bell peppers, chopped
2 sticks celery, thickly sliced
1 pound canned plum tomatoes, chopped and
    sieved
2 tbsps red wine vinegar
1 tbsp sugar
1 clove garlic, crushed
Salt and freshly ground black pepper
12 pitted black olives, quartered
1 tbsp capers

---

1. Cut the eggplant in half lengthwise and score the cut surface deeply, in a lattice fashion, with the point of a sharp knife.

Step 1 Score the cut surface of the eggplants in a lattice pattern, using the point of a sharp knife.

Step 6 Simmer the casserole, uncovered, over a low heat until the juice has thickened and reduced.

2. Sprinkle the cut surface liberally with salt, and leave to stand 30 minutes. Rinse thoroughly under running water, then pat dry and cut it into 1-inch cubes.

3. Heat the oil in a large skillet and add the onion, peppers, and celery. Cook gently about 5 minutes, stirring occasionally, until the vegetables have softened but not browned.

4. Add the eggplant to the pan and mix well to coat thoroughly with the oil. Continue cooking gently 5 minutes.

5. Add the sieved tomatoes to the pan, along with the remaining ingredients, except for the olives and capers. Cover and simmer 5 minutes.

6. Add the olives and capers and continue cooking gently, uncovered, 15 minutes, or until most of the liquid has evaporated and the sauce has thickened and reduced.

Seviche

SERVES 4

In this traditional Mexican dish, the raw fish is "cooked" in a mixture of oil and lime juice.

PREPARATION: 20 mins plus 24 hrs standing time

1 pound fresh cod or red fillet, skinned
Juice and grated rind of 2 limes
1 small shallot, finely chopped
1 green chili, seeded and finely chopped
1 tsp ground coriander
1 small green pepper, sliced
1 small red pepper, sliced
4 green onions (scallions), finely chopped
1 tbsp chopped parsley
1 tbsp chopped coriander (cilantro)
2 tbsps olive oil
Freshly ground black pepper
1 small lettuce, to serve

1. Using a sharp knife, cut the fish into very thin strips across the grain. Put the strips into a large bowl and pour the lime juice over them.

Step 1 Cut the fish fillet across the grain into very thin slices.

Step 3 After refrigerating 24 hours, the fish should have a cooked appearance.

2. Stir in the grated lime rind, shallot, chili, and ground coriander. Mix well.

3. Cover the bowl with plastic wrap and refrigerate 24 hours, stirring occasionally during this time to ensure that the fish remains well-coated with the lime.

4. Mix the sliced peppers, green onions, and the fresh herbs together in a large bowl.

5. Put the fish mixture into a colander and drain off the juice. Add to the pepper mixture and stir in the oil, mixing well to coat evenly. Add freshly ground pepper to taste.

6. Finely shred the lettuce and arrange on a serving platter. Spread the fish mixture attractively over the lettuce and serve immediately, garnished with slices of lime, if wished.

Eggplant Bake

SERVES 6

Eggplants are wonderfully filling vegetables with very few calories – the ideal ingredient in a calorie-controlled diet.

PREPARATION: 30 mins
COOKING: 40 mins

---

2 large or 3 medium-sized eggplants
2 tsps salt
⅔ cup vinegar
2 tbsps vegetable oil
2 large onions, sliced into rings
2 green chilies, seeded and finely chopped
1-pound can chopped tomatoes
½ tsp chili powder
1 tsp crushed garlic
½ tsp ground turmeric
8 tomatoes, sliced
1¼ cups plain low-fat yogurt
1 tsp freshly ground black pepper
½ cup yellow cheese, finely grated

---

1. Cut the eggplants into ¼-inch thick slices. Arrange the slices in a shallow dish and sprinkle with 1 tsp of the salt. Pour over the vinegar, cover and marinate 30 minutes.

2. Drain the eggplants well, discarding the marinade liquid. Press the slices into a colander using the back of your hand, to remove all of the excess vinegar.

3. Heat the oil in a skillet and gently sauté the onion rings until they are golden-brown.

4. Add the chilies, the remaining salt, chopped

Step 7 Spoon half the tomato sauce over the eggplant slices in the gratin dish.

tomatoes, chili powder, garlic, and turmeric. Mix well and simmer 5-7 minutes until thick and well-blended.

5. Remove the sauce from the heat and cool slightly. Blend to a smooth purée in a liquidizer or food processor.

6. Arrange half of the eggplant slices in a lightly-greased shallow, ovenproof dish.

7. Spoon half of the tomato sauce over the eggplant, cover with the remaining eggplant, and then top with the rest of the tomato sauce, and sliced tomatoes.

8. Mix together the yogurt, black pepper, and cheese, and pour this over the tomato slices.

9. Bake in an oven preheated to 375°F, for 20-30 minutes, or until the topping bubbles and turns golden-brown. Serve hot, straight from the oven.

Chicken with 'Broiled' Peppers and Coriander

SERVES 4

'Broiling' peppers is a technique for removing the skins which also imparts a delicious flavor to this popular vegetable.

PREPARATION: 30 mins
COOKING: 1½ hrs

2 red peppers, halved and seeded
1 green pepper, halved and seeded
4 tbsps vegetable oil, for brushing
1 tbsp olive oil
2 tsps paprika
¼ tsp ground cumin
Pinch cayenne pepper
2 cloves garlic, crushed
2 cups canned tomatoes, drained and chopped
3 tbsps fresh chopped coriander (cilantro)
3 tbsps fresh chopped parsley
Salt, for seasoning
4 large chicken breasts, boned
1 large onion, sliced
4 tbsps flaked almonds

1. Put the peppers, cut side down, on a flat surface and gently press them flat. Brush the skin side with 2 tbsps of the vegetable oil and cook them under a hot broiler until the skin chars and splits.

2. Wrap the peppers in a clean kitchen towel for 10 minutes to cool, then carefully peel off the charred skin. Chop the pepper flesh into thin strips.

3. Heat the olive oil in a frying pan and gently fry all the spices and garlic for 2 minutes, stirring to prevent the garlic from browning.

4. Stir in the tomatoes, herbs, and seasoning. Simmer 15-20 minutes, or until thick. Set aside.

5. Heat the remaining vegetable oil in a flameproof casserole or Dutch oven, and sauté the chicken breasts, turning them frequently until golden on both sides.

6. Remove the chicken and set aside. Gently sauté the onion in the oil about 5 minutes, or until softened.

7. Return the chicken to the casserole with the onion and pour on about 1½ cups of water. Bring to the boil. Cover the casserole and simmer about 30 minutes, turning the chicken occasionally to prevent it from burning.

8. Remove the chicken from the casserole and boil the remaining liquid rapidly to reduce to about ⅓ cup of broth. Add the peppers and the tomato sauce, stirring well.

9. Return the chicken to the casserole, cover, and simmer very gently a further 30 minutes, or until tender.

10. Arrange the chicken on a serving platter with a little of the sauce spooned over it. Sprinkle with the flaked almonds and serve any remaining sauce separately.

Herrings with Apples

SERVES 4

The addition of apples beautifully complements the delicious and wholesome flavor of herring.

PREPARATION: 15-20 mins
COOKING: 50 mins

---

4 herrings, cleaned
2 large dessert apples
4 large potatoes, peeled and sliced
1 large onion, thinly sliced
Salt and freshly ground black pepper
⅔ cup cider
½ cup dried breadcrumbs
4 tbsps polyunsaturated margarine
1 tbsp fresh chopped parsley

---

1. Cut the heads and tails from the herrings and split them open from the underside.

2. Put the herrings, belly side down, on a flat surface, and carefully press along the back of each fish with the palm of your hand, pushing the backbone down toward the surface.

3. Turn the herrings over and with a sharp knife, carefully prise away the backbone, pulling out any loose bones as well. Do not cut the fish into separate fillets. Wash and dry them well.

4. Peel, quarter, core, and slice one of the apples. Lightly grease a shallow baking dish and layer the potatoes, apple, and onions, seasoning well with salt and pepper between layers.

Step 3
Carefully lift the backbone away from the fish with a sharp knife, pulling any loose bones out at the same time.

5. Pour the cider over the top potato layer and cover the dish with foil. Bake 40 minutes in a preheated oven at 350°F.

6. Remove the dish from the oven and arrange the fish fillets on the top. Sprinkle the breadcrumbs over them and dot with half of the margarine.

7. Increase the oven temperature to 400°F and return the dish to the oven for about 10-15 minutes, or until the fish are cooked and brown.

8. Core the remaining apple and slice into rounds, leaving the peel on. Melt the remaining margarine in a skillet and gently sauté the apple slices.

9. Remove the fish from the oven and garnish with the sautéed apple slices and chopped parsley. Serve at once.

Veal with Sorrel Stuffing

SERVES 6

*Fresh sorrel has a delightful flavor, but if it is not available use spinach
or silverbeet (Swiss chard).*

PREPARATION: 25 mins
COOKING: 1 hr

---

2 pounds rolled leg of veal
½ cup low fat soft cheese with garlic and herbs
2 cups sorrel, finely chopped
2 tsps fresh oregano or marjoram, chopped
2 tbsps walnuts, finely chopped
Freshly ground black pepper
4 tbsps all-purpose flour
½ tsp paprika
1 egg, beaten
1 cup dried breadcrumbs
3 tbsps polyunsaturated margarine, melted

---

1. Unroll the veal roast and trim some of the fat from the outside, using a sharp knife.

2. Put the cheese, sorrel, oregano or marjoram, walnuts, and black pepper into a bowl. Mix

Step 2 Spread the filling ingredients evenly over the inside of the veal.

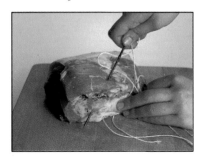

Step 2 Sew the ends of the veal together using a trussing needle and strong thread.

together, using a round-bladed knife or your hands, until the ingredients are well bound together. Spread this filling over the inside of the veal. Roll the veal up, jellyroll fashion, and stitch the ends together with a trussing needle and thick thread.

3. Dredge the veal roll with the flour and sprinkle with the paprika. Press this coating firmly over the meat, using your hands.

4. Brush the floured meat liberally with beaten egg and roll it into the dried breadcrumbs, pressing gently to make sure that all surfaces are thoroughly coated.

5. Place the coated veal in a roasting pan, brush with the melted margarine and roast in a preheated oven at 325°F, for 1 hour, or until the meat is well-cooked.

6. Allow to stand 10 minutes before slicing and serving hot, or chill and serve cold.

Tarragon Broiled Mullet

SERVES 4

Mullet is small fish that is available in the northeast. Porgy or redfish can be substituted

PREPARATION: 10 mins plus marinating
COOKING: 10-16 mins

---

4 large or 8 small red mullet, dressed, scaled, washed and dried
4 or 8 sprigs fresh tarragon
4 tbsps vegetable oil
2 tbsps tarragon vinegar
Salt and freshly ground black pepper

---

1. Rub the inside of each mullet with a teaspoon of salt, scrubbing hard to remove any discolored membranes inside. Rinse thoroughly.

2. Place a sprig of fresh tarragon inside each fish.

Step 1 Rub the insides of each fish with a teaspoon of salt, scrubbing briskly to remove any discolored membranes.

Step 3 Using a sharp knife, cut 2 diagonal slits on the side of each fish, taking great care not to cut right through the flesh.

3. Using a sharp knife cut 2 diagonal slits on both sides of each fish.

4. Mix together the vegetable oil, tarragon vinegar, and a little salt and pepper, in a small bowl.

5. Arrange the fish on a shallow dish and pour the tarragon vinegar marinade over it, brushing some of the mixture into the cuts on the side of the fish. Refrigerate 30 minutes.

6. Arrange the fish on a broiler pan and cook under a preheated hot broiler for 5-8 minutes per side, depending on the size of the fish. Baste frequently with the marinade while cooking. Serve with some sprigs of fresh tarragon, if liked.

Chicken with Lemon Julienne

SERVES 4-6

Lean chicken served with a tangy julienne of fresh vegetables makes a delicious entrée.

PREPARATION: 40 mins
COOKING: 55 mins

---

1 × 3-pound chicken
2 tbsps olive oil
2 tbsps polyunsaturated margarine
2 sticks celery
2 carrots
1 small onion, thinly sliced
1 tbsp chopped fresh basil
1 bayleaf
Juice and grated rind of 2 small lemons
⅔ cup water
Salt and freshly ground black pepper
Lemon slices, for garnish

---

1. Cut the chicken into 8 pieces with a sharp knife or a cook's cleaver, slicing lengthwise down the breastbone and through the backbone to halve it completely.

2. Cut the chicken in half again, slitting between the leg joint diagonally up and around the breast joint. Finally, cut the drumsticks from the leg thigh joint, and the wings from the breast joints. Remove the skin from the chicken by pulling and cutting away with a sharp knife.

3. Heat the oil and margarine in a large skillet. Gently sauté the chicken pieces, turning them frequently to brown evenly. Remove and set aside.

4. Using a sharp knife, cut the celery and carrots into pieces 1½ inches long. Cut these pieces lengthwise into long thin matchsticks.

5. Stir the carrots and celery into the chicken juices, along with the onion. Cook over a gentle heat about 3 minutes or until just beginning to soften but not brown.

6. Stir in the basil, bayleaf, lemon juice, and rind, the water, and salt and pepper. Mix well and cook 2-3 minutes. Add the chicken and bring to the boil.

7. Cover the pan and reduce the heat. Allow the casserole to simmer for about 35-45 minutes, or until the chicken is tender and the juices run clear when the meat is pierced with a sharp knife.

8. Remove the chicken and vegetables to a serving dish and discard the bayleaf.

9. Heat the sauce quickly to thicken if necessary. Spoon the sauce over the chicken and garnish with the lemon slices.

Salmon-Trout with Spinach

SERVES 6-8

PREPARATION: 35-40 mins
COOKING: 40 mins

---

1 × 2½ pound fresh whole salmon-trout,
   cleaned
8 cups spinach, stalks removed
1 small onion, finely chopped
4 tbsps polyunsaturated margarine
4 tbsps walnuts, roughly chopped
1 cup fresh white breadcrumbs
1 tbsp fresh chopped parsley
1 tbsp fresh chopped thyme
¼ tsp grated nutmeg
Salt and freshly ground black pepper
Juice of 2 lemons
Watercress sprigs and lemon slices, to garnish

---

1. Carefully slit the underside of the fish to the tip of the tail. Flatten it, belly side down, on a work surface.

2. Using the palm of your hand press down along the backbone, to push the spine downward. Turn the fish over and using a sharp knife, carefully pull the backbone away, cutting it out with scissors at the base of the head and tail.

3. Pull out any loose bones with a pair of tweezers then set the fish in the center of a large square of lightly-oiled foil.

4. Put the washed spinach into a large saucepan and sprinkle with salt. Do not add any extra water. Cover and cook over a moderate heat about 3 minutes.

5. Turn into a colander and drain well, pressing with a spoon to remove all the excess moisture. Chop very finely, using a sharp knife.

6. Fry the onion gently in 1 tbsp of the margarine until soft. Stir into the spinach along with the walnuts, breadcrumbs, herbs, nutmeg, salt, pepper, and half the lemon juice. Mix well.

7. Push the stuffing firmly into the cavity of the fish, re-shaping it as you do so. Seal the foil over the fish, but do not wrap too tightly. Place in a roasting pan and bake 35 minutes in a preheated oven at 350°F.

8. Carefully unwrap the fish and transfer to a large serving platter. Using a sharp knife, peel away the exposed skin of the fish.

9. Dot with the remaining margarine, sprinkle with the remaining lemon juice, and garnish with watercress and lemon slices.

Lime Roasted Chicken, a tangy, low-calorie dish

AMERICA'S BEST

Chicken

R E C I P E S

Chicken Satay

SERVES 4

This typical Indonesian dish is very spicy.

PREPARATION: 25 mins
COOKING: 15 mins

2 tbsps soy sauce
2 tbsps sesame oil
2 tbsps lime juice
1 tsp ground cumin
1 tsp turmeric powder
2 tsps ground coriander
1 pound chicken breast, cut into 1-inch cubes
2 tbsps peanut oil
1 small onion, minced
1 tsp chili powder
½ cup crunchy peanut butter
1 tsp brown sugar
Lime wedges and coriander leaves, for garnish

1. Put the soy sauce, sesame oil, lime juice, cumin, turmeric, and coriander into a large bowl and mix well.

Step 5 Thread the marinated meat onto 4 large, or 8 small, kebob skewers.

2. Add the cubed chicken to the soy sauce marinade, and stir well to coat the meat evenly.

3. Cover and allow to stand in a refrigerator for at least 1 hour, but preferably overnight.

4. Drain the meat, reserving the marinade.

5. Thread the meat onto 4 large or 8 small skewers and set aside.

6. Heat the peanut oil in a small saucepan and add the onion and chili powder. Cook gently until the onion is slightly softened.

7. Stir the reserved marinade into the oil and onion mixture, along with the peanut butter and brown sugar. Heat gently, stirring constantly, until all the ingredients are well blended.

8. If the sauce is too thick, stir in 2-4 tbsps boiling water.

9. Arrange the skewers of meat on a broiler pan and cook under a preheated moderate broiler 10-15 minutes. After the first 5 minutes of cooking, baste the meat with a little peanut sauce.

10. During the cooking time turn the meat frequently to cook it on all sides and prevent it browning.

11. Garnish with the lime and coriander leaves, and serve the remaining sauce separately.

Terrine of Spinach and Chicken

SERVES 6-8

This superb terrine makes a delicious appetizer.

PREPARATION: 25 mins
COOKING: 1 hr

8 ounces chicken breasts, boned and skinned
2 egg whites
1 cup fresh white breadcrumbs
1 pound fresh spinach, washed
1 tbsp each of fresh, finely-chopped chervil,
 chives and tarragon
Freshly ground black pepper
1¼ cups heavy cream
½ cup finely chopped walnuts
Pinch nutmeg

Step 3 The spinach should be cooked until it is just wilted.

1. Cut the chicken into small pieces.

2. Put the cut chicken, 1 egg white, and half of the breadcrumbs into a food processor. Blend until well mixed.

3. Put the spinach into a large saucepan, cover with a tight-fitting lid, and cook the spinach 3 minutes, or until it has just wilted.

4. Remove the chicken mixture from the food processor and rinse the bowl.

5. Put the spinach into the food processor along with the herbs, the remaining egg white, and breadcrumbs. Blend until smooth.

6. Season the chicken mixture, and add half of the cream. Mix well to blend thoroughly.

7. Add the walnuts, nutmeg, and remaining cream to the spinach and beat well.

8. Line a 1 quart loaf pan with parchment paper. Lightly oil with a little vegetable oil.

9. Pour the chicken mixture into the loaf pan and spread evenly. Carefully pour the spinach mixture over the chicken mixture, and smooth the top.

10. Cover the pan with lightly-oiled aluminum foil and seal tightly around the edges.

11. Stand the pan in a roasting pan and pour enough warm water into the roasting pan to come halfway up the sides. Cook at 325°F for 1 hour, or until firm.

12. Put the terrine into the refrigerator and chill for at least 12 hours.

13. Carefully lift the terrine out of the pan and peel away the paper.

Crumb Fried Chicken

SERVES 6

A tasty dish from Southern Germany.

PREPARATION: 30 mins
COOKING: 40 mins

3-pound chicken
2 eggs, mixed with a pinch of salt
1 cup breadcrumbs
½ cup grated Parmesan cheese
¼ tsp ground ginger
4 tbsps butter or margarine
3 tbsps oil
Lemon and parsley for garnish

---

1. Preheat the oven to 400°F. To joint the chicken, first cut off the legs, bending them backward to break the joint. Cut in between the joint to completely remove the legs.

2. Cut down the breastbone with sharp poultry shears to separate the two halves. Use the poultry shears to cut through the rib cage. Use the notch in the shears to separate the wing

Step 1 Bend the leg backwards to break the ball and socket joint and cut in between.

Step 2 Use the notch to cut through the wing joint.

joints from the back.

3. Cut the quarters into two pieces each. Use a sharp knife to separate the drumstick from the thigh. Cut the breasts in half, leaving some of the white meat attached to the wing joint. Cut through the bones with poultry shears.

4. Mix the breadcrumbs, Parmesan cheese, and ground ginger together. First dip the chicken into the egg and then coat with the crumbs.

5. Heat the oil in a large skillet and add the butter. When hot, add the chicken, skin side down first. Cook both sides until golden brown.

6. Transfer with a slotted spoon to a baking tray and bake in the oven 20-30 minutes, or until the juices run clear when tested with a knife. Serve garnished with small bunches of parsley, and lemon wedges or slices.

Saffron Chicken

SERVES 4

Saffron gives rice and sauces a lovely golden color and delicate taste.

PREPARATION: 20-25 mins
COOKING: 25-35 mins

---

2 tbsps oil
2-3 pound chicken, cut into 8 pieces and
    skinned if desired
1 small onion, finely chopped
2 tsps paprika
1 clove garlic, crushed
8 tomatoes, peeled, seeded and chopped
1¼ cups rice
3 cups boiling water
Large pinch saffron or ¼ tsp ground saffron
¾ cup frozen green peas
2 tbsps chopped parsley

---

1. Heat the oil in a large skillet. Season the chicken and place it in the hot oil, skin side down first. Cook over moderate heat, turning the chicken frequently to brown it lightly. Set the chicken aside.

2. Add the onions to the oil and cook slowly until softened but not colored.

3. Add the paprika and cook about 2 minutes,

Step 4 When the garlic and tomatoes are added, cook over a high heat to evaporate the liquid.

stirring frequently until the paprika loses some of its red color. Add the garlic and the tomatoes.

4. Cook the mixture over high heat about 5 minutes to evaporate the liquid from the tomatoes. The mixture should be of dropping consistency when done. Transfer the mixture to a casserole or Dutch oven, add the rice, water, and saffron and stir together.

5. Add the chicken to the casserole and bring to the boil over high heat. Reduce to simmering, cover tightly, and cook about 20 minutes. Remove chicken, and add the peas and parsley. Cook a further 5-10 minutes, or until rice is tender. Combine with the chicken to serve.

Chicken Cacciatore

SERVES 4-6

A rich Italian dish with mushrooms and olives.

PREPARATION: 30 mins
COOKING: 1hr 15 mins

---

3 tbsps oil
1 cup mushrooms, quartered if large
3 pounds chicken pieces
1 onion
2 cloves garlic
⅔ cup vermouth
1 tbsp white wine vinegar
⅔ cup chicken broth
1 tsp oregano
1 sprig fresh rosemary
1 pound canned tomatoes
¼ cup black olives, pitted
2 tbsps chopped parsley

---

1. Heat the oil in a heavy-based skillet and

Step 3 Cut onion in half lengthwise leaving root end intact. Cut in thin crosswise slices. Then cut in lengthwise strips.

cook the mushrooms about 1-2 minutes. Remove them and set aside.

2. Brown the chicken in the oil and transfer the browned pieces to an ovenproof casserole.

3. Mince the onion and garlic. Pour away all but 1 tbsp of the oil in the skillet and reheat the pan. Cook the onion and garlic until softened but not colored.

4. Add the vermouth and vinegar and boil to reduce by half.

5. Add the chicken broth, tomatoes, oregano, rosemary, and season. Break up the tomatoes and bring the sauce to the boil. Allow to cook 2 minutes.

6. Pour the sauce over the chicken in the casserole, cover, and cook in a preheated 350°F oven about 1 hour.

7. To pit the olives, roll them on a flat surface to loosen the stones and then use a swivel vegetable peeler to extract them. Alternatively use a cherry-pitter.

8. Add mushrooms and olives during the last 5 minutes of cooking.

9. Remove the rosemary before serving and sprinkle with chopped parsley.

Chicken Cobbler

SERVES 6

A warming winter dish with a creamy sauce and biscuit topping.

PREPARATION: 25 mins
COOKING: 1 hr

---

4 chicken pieces, 2 breasts and 2 legs
1½ pints water
1 bayleaf
4 whole peppercorns
2 carrots, peeled and diced
24 pearl onions, peeled
6 tbsps frozen corn kernels
⅔ cup heavy cream

Topping
3½ cups all-purpose flour
1½ tbsps baking powder
Pinch salt
5 tbsps butter or margarine
1½ cups milk
1 egg, beaten with a pinch of salt

---

1. Place the chicken in a deep saucepan or Dutch oven with water, bayleaf, and peppercorns. Cover and bring to the boil. Reduce the heat and allow to simmer 20-30 minutes, or until the chicken is tender. Remove the chicken from the pot and allow to cool. Skim and discard the fat from the surface of the broth. Skin the chicken and remove the meat from the bones.

Step 5 Roll out the mixture on a floured surface, cut into rounds and place on top of the chicken mixture.

2. Continue to simmer the broth until reduced by about half. Strain, then add the carrots and onions. Cook until tender and add the corn. Stir in the cream and season. Add the chicken. Pour into a casserole.

3. To prepare the topping, sift the dry ingredients into a bowl.

4. Rub in the butter or margarine until the mixture resembles small peas. Stir in enough of the milk to bind the mixture.

5. Turn out onto a floured surface and knead lightly. Roll out with a floured rolling pin and cut into rounds with a cookie cutter. Brush the surface of each round with the egg mixture. Place on top of the chicken mixture and bake 10-15 minutes in a pre-heated oven at 375°F. Serve immediately.

Country Captain Chicken

SERVES 6

This dish was named for a sea captain with a taste for the spicy cuisine of India.

PREPARATION: 30 mins
COOKING: 50 mins

3 pounds chicken pieces
Seasoned flour
6 tbsps oil
1 medium onion, chopped
1 medium green bell pepper, seeded and
    chopped
1 clove garlic, crushed
2 tsps curry powder
3½ cups canned tomatoes
2 tsps chopped parsley
1 tsp chopped marjoram
4 tbsps raisins
¼ cup blanched almond halves

1. Remove skin from the chicken and dredge with flour, shaking off the excess.

Step 4 Add the curry powder to the vegetables in the skillet and cook two minutes over low heat, stirring frequently.

Step 5 Toast the almonds on a baking tray in the oven until light golden brown.

2. Heat the oil and brown the chicken on all sides until golden. Remove to an ovenproof casserole.

3. Pour off all but 2 tbsps of the oil. Add the onion, pepper, and garlic and cook slowly to soften.

4. Add the curry powder and season. Cook, stirring frequently, for 2 minutes. Add the tomatoes, parsley, and marjoram and bring to the boil. Pour the sauce over the chicken, cover and cook in a pre-heated 350°F oven for 45 minutes. Add the currants or raisins during the last 15 minutes.

5. Meanwhile, toast the almonds in the oven on a baking tray along with the chicken. Stir them frequently and watch carefully. Sprinkle over the chicken just before serving.

Chicken with Olives

SERVES 4-6

This is a chicken sauté dish for olive lovers. Use more or less of them as your own taste dictates.

PREPARATION: 25 mins
COOKING: 50-55 mins

3 pounds chicken pieces
2 tbsps olive oil
2 tbsps butter or margarine
1 clove garlic, crushed
⅔ cup white wine
⅔ cup chicken stock
2 tbsps chopped parsley
20 pitted black and green olives
4 zucchini, cut in ½-inch pieces

Step 1 Cook the chicken, skin side down first, until golden brown.

To peel a garlic clove easily, first crush it gently with the blunt side of a large knife. The skin will split, making it easier to remove.

1. Heat the oil in a large skillet and add the butter or margarine. When foaming, add the chicken, skin side down. Brown one side of the chicken and turn over to brown the other side. Cook the chicken in two batches if necessary.

2. Turn the chicken skin side up, and add the garlic, wine, and stock, season, then bring to the boil. Cover the pan and allow to simmer over gentle heat about 30-35 minutes.

3. Add the zucchini and cook 10 minutes. Once the chicken and zucchini are done, add the olives and cook to heat through. Add the parsley and remove to a dish to serve.

Chicken with Eggplant and Ham Stuffing

SERVES 4-6

Eggplant and ham make an unusual stuffing and add interest to roast chicken.

PREPARATION: 30 mins
COOKING: 5-6 mins for the stuffing and about
    1 hr for the chicken

3-pound frying chicken
1 small eggplant
4 tbsps butter
1 small onion, finely chopped
½ cup chopped, lean ham
1 cup fresh breadcrumbs
2 tsps dried chopped mixed herbs
1-2 eggs, beaten

---

1. Cut the eggplant in half lengthwise and remove stem. Lightly score the surface with a sharp knife and sprinkle with salt. Leave to stand for about 30 minutes for the salt to draw out any bitter juices.

2. Melt half the butter in a saucepan and cook the onion slowly to soften slightly.

Step 1
Sprinkle the cut surface of the eggplant lightly with salt and leave to stand.

Step 4 Remove the fat from just inside the cavity opening.

3. Rinse the eggplant and pat dry. Cut into ½-inch cubes. Cook with the onion until fairly soft. Add the remaining stuffing ingredients, beating in the egg gradually until the mixture just holds together. Season to taste.

4. Remove the fat from just inside the chicken cavity. Fill the neck end with some of the stuffing. Place any extra in a greased casserole. Tuck the wing tips under the chicken to hold the neck flap down. Tie the legs together and place the chicken in a roasting pan.

5. Spread with the remaining softened butter and roast in a pre-heated 350°F oven for about 1 hour, or until the juices from the chicken run clear when the thickest part of the thigh is pierced with a sharp knife. Cook extra stuffing, covered for the last 35 minutes of cooking time. Leave the chicken to stand for 10 minutes before carving. If desired, make a gravy with the pan juices.

Spicy Spanish Chicken

SERVES 6

Chili peppers, coriander (cilantro) and tomatoes add a Spanish flavor to broiled chicken.

PREPARATION: 1 hr
COOKING: 14-20 mins

---

6 boned chicken breasts
Grated rind and juice of 1 lime
2 tbsps olive oil
6 tbsps whole grain mustard
2 tsps paprika
4 ripe tomatoes, peeled, seeded, and quartered
2 shallots, chopped
1 clove garlic, crushed
½ chili pepper, seeded and chopped
1 tsp wine vinegar
2 tbsps chopped fresh coriander (cilantro)
Whole coriander (cilantro) leaves to garnish

---

1. Place chicken breasts in a shallow dish with the lime rind and juice, oil, mustard, paprika, and coarsely ground black pepper. Marinate

Step 2 Tomatoes peel easily when placed first in boiling water and then in cold.

Step 4 Broil skin side of chicken until brown and crisp before turning pieces over.

about 1 hour, turning occasionally.

2. To peel tomatoes easily, drop them into boiling water for about 5 seconds or less depending on ripeness. Place immediately in cold water. Skins should peel away easily.

3. Coarsely chop tomatoes, shallots, garlic, chili pepper, then add the vinegar and salt. Stir in the coriander (cilantro).

4. Place chicken on a broiler pan and reserve the marinade. Cook chicken, skin side uppermost, about 7-10 minutes, depending on how close the chicken is to the heat source. Baste frequently with the remaining marinade. Broil other side in the same way. Sprinkle with salt after broiling.

5. Place chicken on serving plates and garnish with coriander (cilantro) leaves. Serve with a spoonful of the tomato relish on the side.

Lime Roasted Chicken

SERVES 4

Its simple, tangy flavor make this an ideal summer dish.

PREPARATION: 25 mins, plus 4 hrs to marinate
COOKING: 40 mins

4 chicken breast portions
4 limes
2 tsps white wine vinegar
5 tbsps olive oil
2 tsp fresh chopped basil

1. Rub the chicken portions all over with salt and black pepper. Place in a shallow ovenproof dish, and set aside.

2. Carefully pare away thin strips of the rind from only 2 of the limes, using a lemon parer. Cut these 2 limes in half and squeeze the juice.

3. Add the lime juice to the vinegar and 4 tbsps of the olive oil in a small dish, along with the strips of rind, and mix well.

4. Pour the oil and lime juice mixture over the

Step 5 After marinating for 4 hours, the chicken will look slightly cooked and the meat will have turned a pale opaque color.

Step 7 Sauté the lime slices very quickly in the hot oil until they just begin to soften.

chicken. Cover and refrigerate at least 4 hours or overnight.

5. Remove the covering from the dish in which the chicken is marinating, and baste the chicken well with the marinade mixture. Place in a preheated 375°F oven and cook 30-35 minutes, or until the chicken is well-roasted and tender.

6. In the meantime, peel away the rind and white parts from the remaining 2 limes. Cut the limes into thin slices using a sharp knife.

7. Heat the remaining oil in a small skillet and add the lime slices and basil. Cook quickly 1 minute, or until the fragrance rises up from the basil and the limes just begin to soften.

8. Serve the chicken portions on a serving platter, garnished with the fried lime slices and a little fresh basil.

Chicken and Pepper Salad

SERVES 6

This piquant lunch or light supper dish can be prepared in advance.

PREPARATION: 30 mins

1 pound cooked chicken, cut in strips
⅔ cup mayonnaise
⅔ cup plain yogurt
1 tsp chili powder
1 tsp paprika
Pinch cayenne pepper
½ tsp tomato paste
1 tsp onion paste
1 green bell pepper, seeded and finely sliced
1 red bell pepper, seeded and finely sliced
1 cup frozen sweetcorn, defrosted
1 cup cooked long grain rice

Step 4 Arrange rice on a serving platter and spoon salad into the center.

Step 2 Fold all ingredients together gently so that they do not break up. Use a large spoon or rubber spatula.

1. Place the chicken strips in a large salad bowl.

2. Mix the mayonnaise, yogurt, spices, tomato paste, and onion purée together and leave to stand briefly for flavors to blend. Fold dressing into the chicken.

3. Add the peppers and sweetcorn and mix gently until all the ingredients are coated with dressing.

4. Place the rice on a serving platter and pile the salad into the center. Serve immediately.

Chicken and Avocado Salad

SERVES 4

The creamy herb dressing complements this easy summer salad.

PREPARATION: 30 mins

8 anchovy fillets, soaked in milk, rinsed and dried
1 green onion (scallion), chopped
2 tbsps chopped fresh tarragon
3 tbsps chopped chives
4 tbsps chopped parsley
1¼ cups mayonnaise
⅔ cup plain yogurt
2 tbsps tarragon vinegar
Pinch sugar and cayenne pepper
1 large Boston or iceberg lettuce
1 pound cooked chicken
1 avocado, peeled and cubed
1 tbsp lemon juice

Step 3 Arrange lettuce on individual plates and top with shredded chicken.

Step 1 The dressing should be very well blended after working in a food processor. Alternatively, use a hand blender.

1. Combine all the ingredients, except the lettuce, avocado, and chicken in a food processor. Work the ingredients until smooth, and well mixed. Leave in the refrigerator at least 1 hour for the flavors to blend.

2. Shred the lettuce or tear into bite-size pieces and arrange on plates.

3. Top the lettuce with the cooked chicken cut into strips or cubes.

4. Spoon the dressing over the chicken. Toss the avocado cubes with lemon juice and garnish the salad. Serve any remaining dressing separately.

Tarragon Chicken Pancakes

SERVES 4

These easy-to-make pancakes are sophisticated enough for a dinner party.

PREPARATION: 25 mins
COOKING: 25 mins

Pancake batter
4 ounces wholewheat flour
1 egg
1¼ cups milk
Oil for frying

Filling
3 tbsps all-purpose flour
1¼ cups skim milk
1 cup skinned, chopped cooked chicken
1 avocado, peeled, halved, pitted and chopped
2 tsps lemon juice
1 tbsp chopped fresh tarragon

1. Sift the wholewheat flour into a large bowl, and make a slight well in the center. Break the egg into the well and begin to beat it carefully into the flour, incorporating only a little flour at a time.

2. Add the milk gradually to the egg and flour mixture, beating well between additions, until all the milk is incorporated and the batter is smooth.

3. Heat a little oil in a small skillet, or omelet pan and cook about 2 tbsps of the batter at a time, tipping and rotating the pan, so that the batter spreads evenly over the base to form a

Step 3 Using a small skillet or omelet pan, heat a little oil and fry 2 tbsps of the batter at a time.

pancake. Flip the pancake over, to cook the other side.

4. Repeat this process until all the batter has been used. Keep the pancakes warm until required.

5. Blend the all-purpose flour with a little of the milk, then gradually add the rest of the milk.

6. Pour the flour-and-milk mixture into a small pan, and cook over a moderate heat, stirring continuously, until the sauce has thickened. Season to taste.

7. Stir the chopped chicken, avocado, lemon juice, and tarragon into the sauce.

8. Fold each pancake in half, and then in half again, to form a triangle.

9. Carefully open part of the triangle out to form an envelope, and fill this with the chicken and avocado mixture.

AMERICA'S BEST

Fish &

SEAFOOD

Smoked Mackerel Pâté

SERVES 4

Smoked fish has a wonderful flavor and is ideal for making pâté.
Other oily fish can be used in the same way.

PREPARATION: 30 mins, plus 30 mins chilling

8 smoked mackerel fillets, skin and bones
   removed
4 tbsps margarine
Juice of ½ orange
1 tsp tomato paste
1 tsp white wine vinegar
Salt and freshly ground black pepper, optional
3½ ounces can red pimiento peppers, drained
1¼ cups clear vegetable broth
2 tsps unflavored gelatin
2 tbsps dry sherry
2 tbsps cold water

1. Put the mackerel, margarine, orange juice, tomato paste, vinegar, and seasonings into a

Step 2 Arrange the strips of pimento in a lattice pattern over the top of the pâté.

Step 4 Sprinkle the gelatine over the hot stock and allow it to stand, to dissolve completely.

liquidizer or food processor, and blend until smooth.

2. Put the pâté into a serving dish and smooth the top evenly. Cut the pimientos into thin strips, and arrange in a lattice over the top of the pâté.

3. Bring the broth to the boil in a small pan. Remove from the heat and cool 1 minute.

4. Sprinkle over the gelatin and allow to stand, stirring occasionally until it has completely dissolved. When the liquid is clear, stir in the sherry and cold water.

5. Very carefully spoon the aspic over the top of the pâté and the pimientos, taking great care not to dislodge the lattice pattern. Chill until the aspic has completely set.

Mussels in White Wine

SERVES 3-4

Mussels make a delicious appetizer to a meal and are quick to prepare.

PREPARATION: 20 mins
COOKING: 6-8 mins

---

60 live mussels
1 large onion, or 4 shallots, finely chopped
2 cups dry white wine
2 tsps all-purpose flour
2 tsps butter
Salt and pepper
Pinch of ground nutmeg
2 tbsps chopped parsley

---

1. Wash and scrub the mussels well, discarding any that are open, and will not close when lightly tapped. Place the mussels in a large saucepan, add the onion or shallots, and wine.

2. Cover and bring to the boil. Cook about 5 minutes, shaking the saucepan from time to time, until all the mussels are open. Discard any that have not opened.

3. Strain the liquor into another saucepan. Remove the top shells from the mussels and put the mussels into warmed soup plates; keep warm.

4. Work the flour into the butter and add in small pieces to the strained liquor. Bring to the boil, whisking constantly as it thickens. Season to taste with salt, pepper, and nutmeg. Add the parsley, and pour over the mussels.

Deviled Crabs

SERVES 6
Crab makes an ideal appetizer for a dinner party.

PREPARATION: 35 mins
COOKING: 15 mins

---

6 boiled Dungeness crabs
1 tbsp butter
2 tbsps flour
1 cup heavy cream
2 tsps mustard powder
1 tsp Worcestershire sauce
Salt and pepper
4 hard-cooked eggs
Dry breadcrumbs
Melted butter
Chopped parsley

---

1. Break off all the crab claws. Crack the large claws and legs and pick out the meat. Reserve the smaller legs. Break the crabmeat into pieces and discard any cartilage and shell.

2. Separate the bodies from the large shells. Discard the spongy "fingers" and the stomach, which is found just under the head. Pick out all the meat and combine it with the claw meat. Clean the upper shells thoroughly.

3. Melt the butter and add the flour, stirring well. Stir in the cream, mustard, and Worcestershire sauce. Cook over moderate heat, stirring constantly, until thickened. Add salt and pepper to taste.

4. Chop the hard-cooked eggs and add to the sauce with the crabmeat. Spoon into the clean shells, sprinkle lightly with breadcrumbs, and drizzle with melted butter.

5. Bake in an oven preheated to 350°F about 10 minutes, or until golden-brown. Sprinkle with some chopped parsley, and serve surrounded by the reserved crab legs.

Taramasalata

SERVES 4

This classic Greek appetizer is a delicious way of improving your intake of vitamins B and C.

PREPARATION: 15-25 mins, plus 30 mins chilling

3 ounces smoked fish roe
6 slices white bread, crusts removed
Juice of 1 lemon
1 small onion, finely chopped
6 tbsps olive oil
Black olives and chopped fresh parsley, for garnish

1. Cut the fish roe in half and scrape out the center into a bowl. Discard the skin.

2. Put the bread into a bowl along with ⅔ cup warm water. Allow the bread to soak about 10 minutes, then drain off the water, and squeeze the bread until it is almost dry. Add the bread to

Step 2 Allow the bread to soak for about 10 minutes, then drain off the water, squeeze the bread until it is almost dry.

Step 4 Gradually add the oil to the fish mixture, beating continuously between additions, to prevent curdling.

the bowl containing the roe, and stir in with the lemon juice.

3. Put the cod roe mixture into a blender or food processor, along with the onion. Process until the ingredients form a smooth paste.

4. Return the blended mixture to a bowl and gradually beat in the oil, a little at a time, as if making mayonnaise. Beat the mixture very thoroughly between additions, with a whisk or wooden spoon.

5. Refrigerate for at least 30 minutes to chill thoroughly, then transfer to a serving bowl, and garnish with the black olives and chopped parsley.

Sole Surprise

Serve these tasty fish parcels with new potatoes and broccoli.

PREPARATION: 25 mins
COOKING: 40 mins

---

8 ounces puff dough
2 cups frozen spinach, defrosted
4 tbsps butter
4 small or 2 large fillets of sole, skinned

Sauce
2 tbsps butter
2 tbsps all-purpose flour
1½ cups milk
Pinch of dried dill
Salt and pepper
½ cup shredded yellow cheese

---

1. Roll the dough out into a rectangle 5×8 inches. Cut into four equal-size rectangles 2½×4 inches.

2. Fold the rectangles over, short sides together. Cut out the centers with a sharp knife, leaving ½ inch all round. Roll out the center pieces on a floured board until they are the same size as the "frames."

3. Brush the edges with milk and put the "frames" on the base. Brush the tops with milk and place on a greased baking tray. Bake in an oven preheated to 425°F 10-15 minutes, or until well risen and golden-brown.

4. Meanwhile, put the spinach in a pan with ¼ inch water and a little salt. Cover and cook 4-5 minutes. Drain well and beat in half the butter.

5. Skin the fish fillets and cut in two if necessary. Use the rest of the butter to coat two heatproof-platters and put the fillets on one and cover them with the other. Place the platters over a pan of boiling water and steam 20 minutes or until the fish is cooked through.

6. For the sauce, melt the butter then stir in the flour to make a roux. Gradually stir in the milk. Bring to the boil. Reduce the heat and season. Cook 1 minute, remove from the heat, and stir in the cheese.

7. Cut out the puffed inside of the pastry "boxes" and use for lids. Divide the spinach between the boxes, lay the sole on top, and add the sauce.

Singapore Fish

SERVES 6

The cuisine of Singapore was much influenced by that of China. In turn, the Chinese brought ingredients like curry powder into their own cuisine.

PREPARATION: 25 mins
COOKING: 10 mins

6 white fish fillets
1 egg white
1 tbsp cornstarch
2 tsps white wine
Salt and pepper
Oil for frying
1 large onion, cut into ½-inch thick wedges
1 tbsp mild curry powder
1 small can pineapple pieces, drained, juice reserved
1 small can mandarin orange segments, drained and juice reserved
1 tbsp cornstarch mixed with juice of 1 lime
2 tsps sugar (optional)
1 small can sliced water chestnuts, drained
Pinch salt and pepper

1. Starting at the tail end of the fillets, skin them using a sharp knife. Hold the knife at an angle and, using a sawing motion, cut along the length of each fillet, pushing the fish flesh along as you go. Cut the fish into even-sized pieces, about 2 inches.

2. Mix together the egg white, cornstarch, wine, salt, and pepper. Place the fish in the mixture, and leave to stand while heating the oil in a wok or skillet.

Step 1 Hold a filleting knife at a slight angle and slide the knife along the length of the fillet in a sawing motion.

3. When the oil is hot, fry a few pieces of fish at a time until light golden-brown and crisp. Remove the fish to kitchen paper to drain.

4. Remove all but 1 tbsp of the oil from the wok or skillet and add the onion. Stir-fry 1-2 minutes and add the curry powder. Cook for a further 1-2 minutes. Add the juice from the pineapple and mandarin oranges, and bring to the boil.

5. Combine the cornstarch and lime juice, and add a spoonful of the boiling fruit juice. Add the mixture to the wok or skillet and cook until thickened, about 2 minutes. Taste and add sugar if required. Add the fruit, water chestnuts, seasoning, and fried fish to the wok, and stir to coat. Heat through 1 minute and serve immediately.

Snapper with Fennel-and-Orange Salad

SERVES 4

This makes a lovely summer meal. Substitute other white fish if you can't get snapper.

PREPARATION: 30 mins
COOKING: 6-10 mins

Oil
4 even-sized red snapper, cleaned
2 bulbs fennel
2 oranges
Juice of 1 lemon
3 tbsps olive oil
Pinch sugar, salt, and black pepper

---

1. Brush the fish all over with oil, and cut three slits into both sides of each. Sprinkle with a little of the lemon juice.

2. Core the fennel then slice thinly. Slice the

Step 2 Slice the fennel in half and remove the cores.

Step 3 Segment the oranges over a bowl to catch the juice.

green tops and chop the feathery fronds to use in the dressing.

3. Using a sharp knife, cut off all the peel and white parts from the oranges. Cut the flesh into segments, slicing in between the membranes. Hold the fruit over a bowl to catch the juice.

4. Add the rest of the lemon juice to the orange juice in the bowl. Add the oil and seasonings. Mix well and add the fennel, green tops, and orange segments, stirring carefully.

5. Cook the fish under a preheated medium hot broiler 3-5 minutes per side, depending on thickness. The flesh will flake easily when it is cooked. Serve with the salad.

Seafood Torta

SERVES 6-8

A very stylish version of a fish quiche, this makes a perfect lunch with some salad.

PREPARATION: 40 mins, plus chilling time
COOKING: 40 mins

Pastry
2 cups all-purpose flour, sifted
Pinch salt
½ cup unsalted butter
4 tbsps cold milk

Filling
4 white fish fillets
⅔ cup water
⅔ cup white wine
Large pinch dried red pepper flakes
1 cup cooked bay shrimp
½ cup crabmeat
2 tbsps butter
2 tbsps flour
1 clove garlic, crushed
2 egg yolks
⅔ cup heavy cream
1 tbsp chopped fresh parsley

1. To prepare the dough, sift the flour and salt into a bowl. Rub in the butter, until the mixture resembles breadcrumbs. Pour in the milk, and mix with a fork to a dough. Form a ball and knead about 1 minute. Chill about 1 hour.

2. To prepare the filling, cook the fish in the water and wine with the pepper flakes about 10 minutes or until just firm. Remove from the liquid and flake into a bowl. Add the shrimp and crab. Reserve the cooking liquid.

3. Melt the butter in a saucepan and stir in the flour. Gradually strain on the cooking liquid, stirring constantly until smooth. Add garlic, place over high heat, and bring to the boil; cook 1 minute. Add to the fish and set aside to cool.

4. Roll out the dough and use to line a loose-bottomed quiche or pie pan. Prick lightly with a fork and chill 30 minutes. Place parchment paper inside the case and fill with rice or baking beans. Bake 15 minutes in an oven preheated to 375°F.

5. Combine the egg yolks, cream, and parsley, and stir into the filling. When the pastry is ready, remove the paper and beans, and pour in the filling.

6. Bake a further 25 minutes. Allow to cool slightly and remove from the pan.

Skate Wings with Butter Sauce

SERVES 4

Skate wings are both economical and delicious, and make an interesting change from everyday fish dishes. Other flatfish can be used.

PREPARATION: 10-15 mins
COOKING: 20 mins

---

4 skate wings
1 very small onion, sliced
2 parsley sprigs
6 black peppercorns
1¼ cups vegetable or fish broth
4 tbsps unsalted butter
1 tbsps capers
2 tbsps white wine vinegar
1 tbsp fresh chopped parsley

---

1. Place the skate wings in one layer in a large, deep skillet. Add the onion slices, parsley, and peppercorns, then pour over the broth.

Step 3 Carefully remove any skin or large bones from the cooked fish, using a small sharp, pointed knife.

Step 4 Add the vinegar to the hot butter and capers. This will cause the butter to foam.

2. Bring gently to the boil with the pan uncovered, and allow to simmer for 10-15 minutes, or until the fish is cooked and tender.

3. Carefully remove the skate wings from the pan, and arrange on a serving platter. Remove any skin or large pieces of bone, taking great care not to break up the fish. Keep warm.

4. Place the butter into a small pan, and cook over a high heat until it begins to brown. Add the capers, and immediately remove the butter from the heat. Stir in the vinegar to make the hot butter foam.

5. Pour the hot butter sauce over the skate wings and sprinkle with some chopped parsley. Serve immediately.

Stuffed Sole

SERVES 6

This German dish is elegant enough for a formal dinner party.

PREPARATION: 30 mins
COOKING: 20-30 mins

½ cup butter
2 tbsps flour
2 cups fish or vegetable broth
¾ cup button mushrooms, sliced
4 tbsps heavy cream
2 tbsps brandy
½ cup cooked, peeled shrimp
½ cup canned, frozen or fresh crabmeat
2 tbsps fresh breadcrumbs
Salt and pepper
6-12 sole fillets, depending upon size, skinned

---

1. Melt half the butter in a saucepan. Stir in the flour, and cook about 2 minutes over gentle heat or until pale straw-colored. Stir in the broth and bring to the boil. Add the mushrooms, and allow to cook until the sauce thickens.

2. Add the cream and re-boil the sauce.

Step 3 Spread stuffing on one side of each fillet and roll up. Secure with cocktail sticks.

Remove the sauce from the heat, and stir in the brandy, shrimp, crab, breadcrumbs, and salt and pepper.

3. Cut the fish fillets in half lengthwise and spread the filling on the side of the fish that was skinned. Roll the fish up and secure with cocktail sticks.

4. Arrange in a buttered baking dish, and dot the remaining butter over the top. Cook in an oven preheated to 350°F, 20-30 minutes, until the fish is just firm.

Baked Stuffed Mackerel

SERVES 4

In this recipe the combination of thyme and parsley in the stuffing beautifully complements the flavor of the mackerel. Herrings would also work well with the combination.

PREPARATION: 10 mins
COOKING: 25-30 mins

4 tbsps butter
1 small onion, minced
1 tbsp raw oatmeal
½ cup breadcrumbs
2 tsps freshly chopped thyme or ½ tsp dried
2 tsps freshly chopped parsley or ½ tsp dried
Salt and pepper
2-3 tbsps hot water
4 mackerel, well-cleaned and washed
1 lemon, sliced, for garnish

1. Heat the butter in a skillet, add the onion, and sauté to soften. Add the oatmeal, breadcrumbs, herbs, and seasoning. Mix well, then bind together with the hot water.

2. Fill the cavities of the fish with the stuffing and wrap each one separately in well-buttered foil.

3. Place the parcels in a roasting-pan or on a baking tray and bake in an oven preheated to 375°F 25-30 minutes or until cooked through and firm to the touch. Serve with lemon slices and thyme.

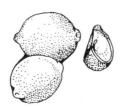

Swedish Mackerel

SERVES 4

The Swedes adore the flavor of fresh dill and mild mustard. This combination is all that is required to bring out the full flavor of fresh mackerel.

PREPARATION: 10 mins
COOKING: 10-12 mins

---

4 tbsps fresh chopped dill
6 tbsps mild mustard
2 tbsps lemon juice or white wine
4-8 fresh mackerel, cleaned
2 tbsps unsalted butter, melted
Freshly ground black pepper
Lemon wedges and whole sprigs of fresh dill,
   to garnish

---

1. Put the dill, mustard, and lemon juice or white wine into a small bowl, and mix together thoroughly.

2. Using a sharp knife, cut three shallow slits

Step 2 Using a very sharp knife, cut 3 shallow slits just through the skin on each side of the fish.

Step 3 Spread the mustard mixture over each fish, carefully pushing a little into each cut.

through the skin on both sides of each fish.

3. Spread half of the mustard mixture over one side of each fish, pushing some of the mixture into each cut.

4. Drizzle a little of the melted butter over the fish, and cook under a preheated hot broiler 5-6 minutes.

5. Using a metal spatula, carefully turn each fish over, and spread with the remaining dill and mustard mixture.

6. Sprinkle with the remaining butter and broil a further 5-6 minutes, or until the fish is thoroughly cooked.

7. Sprinkle the fish with black pepper, and serve garnished with dill sprigs and lemon wedges.

Swordfish with Garlic Sauce

SERVES 4

Swordfish steaks are delicious and are now easily available throughout the country.

PREPARATION: 25 mins plus overnight
    marinating
COOKING: 10-15 mins

---

2 tbsps fresh green peppercorns
6 tbsps lemon juice
4 tbsps olive oil
Freshly ground sea or kosher salt
4 swordfish steaks
1 egg
1 clove garlic, coarsley chopped
⅔ cup oil
2 sprigs fresh oregano leaves, finely chopped
Salt and freshly ground black pepper

---

1. Crush the green peppercorns lightly, using a pestle and mortar. Mix together the lemon juice, olive oil, and salt.

2. Place the swordfish steaks in a shallow,

Step 1 Lightly crush the green peppercorns using a pestle and mortar.

Step 3
Marinate the swordfish steaks overnight, after which they should be opaque.

ovenproof dish and pour the lemon and oil mixture over each steak. Refrigerate overnight, turning occasionally until the fish becomes opaque.

3. Using a blender or food processor, mix together the egg and garlic.

4. With the machine still running, gradually pour the oil through the funnel in a thin, steady stream onto the egg and garlic mixture. Continue to blend until the sauce is thick.

5. Preheat a broiler to hot and arrange the swordfish on the broiler pan, sprinkle with the oregano and season well. Cook 10-15 minutes under a preheated hot broiler, turning them frequently, and basting with the lemon-and-pepper marinade.

6. When the steaks are cooked, place on a serving dish, and spoon the garlic mayonnaise over them to serve.

Fish Milanese

SERVES 4

These fish, cooked in the style of Milan, have a crispy crumb coating and the fresh tang of lemon juice.

PREPARATION: 10 mins plus 1 hr marinating
COOKING: 6 mins

---

4 large or 8 white fish fillets, skinned
2 tbsps dry vermouth
6 tbsps olive oil
1 bayleaf
Seasoned flour, for dredging
2 eggs, lightly beaten
Dry breadcrumbs
Oil for shallow frying
6 tbsps butter
1 clove garlic, crushed
2 tsps chopped parsley
1 tsp chopped fresh oregano
2 tbsps capers
Juice of 1 lemon
Salt and pepper
Lemon wedges and parsley, to garnish

Step 3 Dip or brush the fillets with the beaten egg and press on the breadcrumb coating firmly.

1. Place the fish fillets in a large, shallow dish. Combine the vermouth, oil, and bayleaf in a small saucepan and heat gently. Allow to cool completely and pour over the fish. Leave the fish to marinate about 1 hour, turning them occasionally.

2. Remove the fish from the marinade, and dredge lightly with the seasoned flour.

3. Dip the fillets into the beaten eggs to coat, then into the breadcrumbs, pressing the crumbs on firmly.

4. Heat the oil in a large skillet. Add the fillets and cook slowly for about 3 minutes on each side, until golden-brown. Remove and drain on kitchen paper.

5. Drain the oil from the skillet and wipe it clean. Add the butter and the garlic, and cook until both turn a light brown.

6. Add the herbs, capers, lemon juice, and seasoning and pour immediately over the fish. Garnish with lemon wedges and sprigs of parsley.

Spaghetti with Tomato, Salami and Green Olives

AMERICA'S BEST

Pasta

R E C I P E S

Minestra

SERVES 4-6

A wholesome soup which makes an ideal starter.

PREPARATION: 15 mins
COOKING: 45 mins

---

4 ounces short-cut macaroni
2 tbsps olive oil
1 onion
1 carrot
1 stick celery
3 pints water
2 cups fresh spinach
2 tomatoes
1 tsp rosemary
2 tbsps chopped parsley
2 cloves garlic, crushed
4 tbsps Parmesan cheese, grated
Salt and pepper

Step 4 Add the shredded spinach leaves to the soup.

1. Cut onion, carrot, and celery into thick matchstick strips.

2. Heat oil in a large, heavy skillet, and fry vegetable strips until just browning, stirring occasionally.

3. Pour on water, add salt and pepper, and simmer 20 minutes.

4. Meanwhile, wash and cut spinach leaves into shreds, add to soup and cook 10 minutes.

5. Scald and skin tomatoes, and chop roughly, removing seeds.

6. Add tomatoes, macaroni, garlic, parsley, and rosemary to the soup, and simmer a further 10 minutes.

7. Adjust seasoning. Serve with grated Parmesan cheese.

Step 1 Cut onion, carrot, and celery into thick matchstick strips.

Tagliatelle Carbonara

SERVES 4

Bacon, cream, and eggs combine to make a rich pasta sauce.

PREPARATION: 10 mins
COOKING: 15 mins

---

10 ounces tagliatelle
2 tbsps butter or margarine
4 Canadian bacon slices, chopped
1 tbsp olive oil
4 tbsps single cream
Pinch of paprika
4 tbsps Parmesan cheese, grated
2 eggs
Salt and pepper

Step 4 Beat together eggs and grated cheese.

Step 7 Add bacon mixture and egg mixture, and toss together.

1. Heat the oil in a skillet, and cook the bacon over a moderate heat until just browning.

2. Add the paprika and cook 1 minute.

3. Add the cream, and stir.

4. Beat together the eggs and grated cheese.

5. Cook the tagliatelle in lots of boiling, salted water 10 minutes, or until tender but still firm.

6. Drain the pasta, return to pan with butter and black pepper, and toss.

7. Add bacon mixture and egg mixture, and toss together. Add salt to taste. Serve immediately.

Spaghetti with Tomato, Salami, and Green Olives

SERVES 4

This robust pasta dish is ideal for a quick supper or light lunch.

PREPARATION: 15 mins
COOKING: 15 mins

10 ounces spaghetti
1 x 14-ounce can plum tomatoes
10 slices salami
1 cup green olives, pitted and chopped
1 clove garlic, crushed
2 tbsps olive oil
½ tbsp oregano
4 tbsps grated pecorino cheese
Salt and pepper

Step 1 Purée tomatoes and push through a sieve into a saucepan.

Step 2 Add oregano, salami, and olives, and heat gently.

1. Purée tomatoes, and push through a sieve into a saucepan.

2. Add oregano, salami, and olives, and heat gently.

3. Add salt and pepper to taste.

4. Meanwhile, cook spaghetti in plenty of boiling, salted water 10 minutes. Drain well.

5. Heat olive oil, garlic, and freshly-ground black pepper in the pan used to cook the spaghetti.

6. Add spaghetti, and pour the sauce over it. Toss well and serve with pecorino cheese.

Pasta with Fresh Tomato and Basil Sauce

SERVES 4

Fresh tomato and basil make a classic sauce for pasta.

PREPARATION: 15-20 mins
COOKING: 10-15 mins

---

1 small onion, finely chopped
1 pound fresh tomatoes
2 tbsps tomato paste
1 orange
2 cloves garlic, crushed
Salt and freshly ground black pepper
⅔ cup red wine
⅔ cup chicken broth
2 tbsps coarsely-chopped basil
12 ounces wholewheat pasta

---

1. Peel and mince the onion.

2. Cut a small cross in the skins of the tomatoes and plunge them into boiling water 30 seconds. Remove and carefully peel away the loosened skin.

3. Cut the tomatoes into quarters, and remove and discard the seeds. Chop the tomato flesh roughly, and put this, the onion, and the tomato paste into a large saucepan.

4. Heat the onion and tomatoes over a gentle heat, stirring continuously until the tomatoes soften and begin to lose their juice.

Step 1 To chop an onion finely, pierce the peeled onion with a fork and use this to hold the vegetable steady whilst you chop.

5. Finely grate the rind from the orange. Cut the orange in half and squeeze out the juice.

6. Put the orange rind and juice into a large saucepan along with all the remaining ingredients, and bring to the boil.

7. Continue to boil until the sauce has reduced and thickened and the vegetables are soft.

8. Whilst the sauce is cooking, put the pasta into another saucepan with enough boiling water to cover. Season with a little salt and cook 10-15 minutes, or until the pasta is soft.

9. Drain the pasta in a colander, and stir it into the hot sauce. Serve at once with a salad.

Tagliatelle with Garlic and Oil

SERVES 4

Garlic and oil combine to make the simplest of pasta sauces.

PREPARATION: 5 mins
COOKING: 10 mins

---

10 ounces green tagliatelle
⅔ cup olive oil
3 cloves garlic, crushed
2 tbsps chopped parsley
Salt and pepper

Step 5 Toss the tagliatelle in the sauce to coat well.

Step 5 Add sauce to tagliatelle.

1. Cook the tagliatelle in lots of boiling, salted water 10 minutes, or until tender but still firm, stirring occasionally.

2. Meanwhile, heat the oil in a skillet and, when warm, add peeled, crushed garlic.

3. Fry gently until golden-brown.

4. Add chopped parsley, and salt and pepper to taste.

5. Drain tagliatelle. Add sauce, and toss to coat well. Serve hot.

Home-made Tagliatelle with Summer Sauce

SERVES 4

Home-made pasta is in a class by itself.

PREPARATION: 30 mins
COOKING: 5-6 mins

Pasta Dough
1 cup all-purpose flour
1 cup fine farina (Cream of Wheat)
2 large eggs
2 tsps olive oil
Pinch salt

Sauce
1 pound unpeeled tomatoes, seeded, and cut
  into small dice
1 large green bell pepper, cored, seeded, and
  cut in small dice
1 onion, cut in small dice
1 tbsp chopped fresh basil
1 tbsp chopped fresh parsley
2 cloves garlic, crushed
⅔ cup olive oil and vegetable oil mixed

1. Place the flour and farina in a mound on a work surface and make a well in the center. Place the eggs, oil, and salt in the center of the well.

2. Using a fork, beat the ingredients in the center to blend them and gradually incorporate the flour from the outside edge.

3. When half the flour is incorporated, start

Step 4 Roll the dough out thinly and cut into thin strips.

kneading, using the palms of the hands and not the fingers. Cover the dough and leave it to rest 15 minutes.

4. Divide the dough into quarters and roll out thinly with a rolling-pin on a floured surface or use a pasta machine, dusting dough lightly with flour before rolling. Allow the sheets of pasta to dry about 10 minutes on a floured surface. Cut the sheets into strips about ¼ inch wide by hand or machine, dusting lightly with flour while cutting. Leave the cut pasta to dry while preparing the sauce.

5. Combine all the sauce ingredients, mixing well. Cover and refrigerate overnight.

6. Cook the pasta 5-6 minutes in boiling, salted water with a spoonful of oil. Drain the pasta and rinse under very hot water. Toss in a colander to drain excess water. Place in a serving dish and coat with the cold sauce.

Penne with Ham and Asparagus

SERVES 4

The Italian word penne means quills, due to the diagonal cut on both ends.

PREPARATION: 20 mins
COOKING: 10 mins

---

8 ounces penne
12 ounces fresh asparagus
4 ounces cooked ham
2 tbsps butter or margarine
1¼ cup heavy cream
4 tbsps grated Parmesan cheese (optional)

---

1. Using a swivel vegetable peeler, scrape the sides of the asparagus spears starting about 2 inches from the top. Cut off the ends of the spears about 1 inch from the bottom.

2. Cut the ham into strips about ½ inch thick.

3. Bring a sauté pan of salted water to the boil. Move the pan so it is half on and half off direct

Step 1 Peel the asparagus stalks with a swivel vegetable peeler.

Step 4 Cut ham and cooked asparagus into 1-inch lengths. Leave the asparagus tips whole.

heat. Place in the asparagus spears so that the tips are off the heat. Cover and bring back to the boil. Cook the asparagus spears about 2 minutes. Drain and allow to cool.

4. Cut the asparagus into 1 inch lengths, leaving the tips whole.

5. Melt the butter in the sauté pan and add the asparagus and ham. Cook briefly to evaporate the liquid, and add the cream. Bring to the boil and cook about 5 minutes to thicken the cream.

6. Meanwhile, cook the pasta in boiling, salted water with a little oil for about 10-12 minutes.

7. Drain the pasta and rinse under hot water. Toss in a colander to drain and mix with the sauce. Serve with grated Parmesan cheese, if desired.

Spaghetti Amatriciana

SERVES 4

Chili pepper brings a fiery taste to this pasta sauce.

PREPARATION: 20-25 mins
COOKING: 10-12 mins

---

1 onion
6 slices smoked bacon
1 pound ripe tomatoes
1 red chili pepper
1½ tbsps oil
12 ounces spaghetti

---

1. Slice the onion thinly. Remove rind from the bacon and cut into thin strips.

2. Drop the tomatoes into boiling water for 6-8 seconds. Remove and place in cold water, and leave to cool. This will make the peels easier to remove.

3. When the tomatoes are peeled, cut them in half and remove the seeds and pulp with a

Step 2 Placing tomatoes in boiling water and then in cold water water makes the skins easier to remove.

Step 4 Remove the stem, seeds, and core from the chili pepper, cut into thin strips and then chop into fine dice.

teaspoon. Chop the tomato flesh roughly and set it aside.

4. Cut the chili pepper in half lengthwise. Remove the seeds and core, and cut the pepper into thin strips. Cut the strips into small dice.

5. Heat the oil in a sauté pan and add the onion and bacon. Stir over medium heat about 5 minutes, until the onion is transparent. Drain off excess fat and add the tomatoes and chili. Mix well. Simmer the sauce gently, uncovered, about 5 minutes, stirring occasionally.

6. Meanwhile, cook the spaghetti in boiling, salted water with a little oil about 10-12 minutes. Drain and rinse in hot water and toss in a colander to dry. To serve, spoon the sauce on top of the spaghetti, and sprinkle with freshly-grated Parmesan cheese.

Spirali with Spinach and Bacon

SERVES 4

Pasta doesn't have to have a sauce that cooks for hours.
This whole dish takes about 20 minutes. True Italian "fast food"!

PREPARATION: 10 mins
COOKING: 10 mins

---

12 ounces pasta spirals
2 cups fresh spinach
3 slices bacon
1 clove garlic, crushed
1 small red or green chili pepper
1 small red sweet pepper
1 small onion
3 tbsps olive oil
Salt and pepper

---

1. Cook the pasta in boiling, salted water about 10-12 minutes or until just tender. Drain in a colander and rinse. Keep the pasta in a bowl of water until ready to use.

Step 2 Tear stalks off the spinach and wash the leaves well.

Step 4 Roll up the leaves in several layers to shred them faster.

2. Tear the stalks off the spinach and wash the leaves well, changing the water several times. Set aside to drain.

3. Remove the rind from the bacon and dice the bacon finely. Cut the chili and the red pepper in half, remove the stems, core and seeds, and slice finely. Slice the onion thinly.

4. Shred the spinach finely.

5. Heat the oil in a sauté pan and add garlic, onion, peppers, and bacon. Fry 2 minutes, add the spinach and fry a further 2 minutes, stirring continuously. Season with salt and pepper.

6. Drain the pasta spirals and toss them in a colander to remove excess water. Mix with the spinach sauce and serve immediately.

Gianfottere Salad

SERVES 4

This delicious Italian salad makes the most of summer vegetables.

PREPARATION: 30 mins
COOKING: 30 mins

---

1 small eggplant
2 tomatoes
1 large zucchini
1 red bell pepper
1 green bell pepper
1 medium onion
1 clove garlic, peeled
4 tbsps olive oil
Salt and pepper
1 pound wholewheat pasta spirals

---

1. Cut the eggplant into ½-inch slices. Sprinkle with salt and leave 30 minutes.

2. Chop the tomatoes roughly and remove the cores.

3. Cut the zucchini into ½-inch slices.

Step 1 Cut the eggplant into ½-inch slices and sprinkle with plenty of salt.

Step 8 Add the eggplant, zucchini, peppers, tomatoes, and garlic to the onion in the skillet.

4. Core and seed the peppers, and chop them roughly

5. Chop the onion. Crush the garlic.

6. Heat 3 tbsps olive oil in a skillet, and sauté the onion gently, until it is transparent.

7. Rinse the salt from the eggplant and pat dry. Chop the eggplant roughly.

8. Stir the eggplant, zucchini, peppers, tomatoes, and garlic into the onion, and fry gently 20 minutes. Season to taste, and allow to cool completely.

9. Cook the pasta spirals in plenty of boiling, salted water for 10-15 minutes.

10. Rinse the pasta in cold water and drain well.

11. Put the pasta into a large mixing bowl, and stir in the remaining olive oil.

12. Stir in the vegetables, mixing well.

Tuna and Tomato Salad

SERVES 4

Serve this salad as part of a summer lunch with a green salad and French bread.

PREPARATION: 10 mins
COOKING: 15 mins

---

1 tbsp chopped fresh basil or marjoram
6 tbsps French dressing
12 ounces pasta spirals
6 tomatoes
1½ cups canned tuna, drained

---

1. Mix the basil or marjoram, with the French dressing.

2. Cook the pasta in a large saucepan of boiling, lightly salted water about 10 minutes.

3. Rinse in cold water and drain well, shaking off any excess water.

4. Put the pasta into a large bowl and toss with

Step 4 Mix the pasta spirals with 3 tbsps of the French dressing in a large bowl.

Step 7 Add the tuna to the pasta and mix together gently.

3 tablespoons of the French dressing, mixing well to ensure that they are evenly coated. Leave to cool.

5. Slice enough of the tomatoes to arrange around the outside of the serving dish and then chop the rest.

6. Put the chopped tomatoes into another bowl and pour the remaining French dressing over them. Arrange this in the center of a serving dish.

7. Add the flaked tuna to the pasta and toss together gently.

8. Pile the pasta and tuna over the chopped tomatoes in the center of the dish.

9. Arrange the tomato slices around the edge of the serving dish, and chill well until required.

Mushroom Pasta Salad

SERVES 4

The piquant lemon marinade brings zest to this easy salad.

PREPARATION: 10 mins, plus 1 hr to marinate the mushrooms
COOKING: 15 mins

---

5 tbsps olive oil
Juice of 2 lemons
1 tsp fresh chopped basil
1 tsp fresh chopped parsley
Salt and pepper
2 cups mushrooms
8 ounces wholewheat pasta shapes

---

1. Mix together the olive oil, lemon juice, herbs, and seasoning.

Step 2 Use a sharp knife to slice the mushrooms thinly.

Step 6 Stir the cooled pasta into the marinated mushrooms, mixing well to coat evenly.

2. Finely slice the mushrooms and add these to the lemon dressing in the bowl, stirring well.

3. Cover the bowl and allow to stand in a cool place for at least 1 hour.

4. Cook the pasta in boiling, salted water 10-15 minutes.

5. Rinse the pasta in cold water and drain well.

6. Add the pasta to the marinated mushrooms and lemon dressing, mixing well to coat evenly.

7. Adjust the seasoning if necessary, then chill well before serving.

Macaroni Cheese with Frankfurters

SERVES 4

A hearty family supper dish, ideal for cold winter evenings.

PREPARATION: 10 mins
COOKING: 20 mins

8 frankfurters or wieners
1 pound macaroni
4 tbsps butter or margarine
¾ cup all-purpose flour
2¼ cups milk
¾ cup grated yellow cheese
1 tsp dry mustard powder
Salt and pepper

1. Poach the sausages 5-6 minutes in slightly salted, boiling water.

2. Remove the skins from the sausages and, when cold, slice diagonally.

3. Cook the macaroni in plenty of boiling, salted water for about 10-15 minutes.

Step 2 Remove the skins from the sausages and cut them diagonally into slices about 1 inch long.

Step 6 Add the milk gradually, beating the mixture well between additions, until all the milk is incorporated.

4. Rinse in cold water and drain well.

5. Melt the butter in a saucepan. Stir in the flour and cook 1 minute.

6. Remove the pan from the heat and add the milk gradually, beating thoroughly and returning the pan to the heat to cook between additions. When all the milk has been added, simmer 2 minutes, stirring occasionally.

7. Stir in the sausages, grated cheese, and mustard. Season to taste.

8. Add the drained macaroni to the sauce and stir well until heated through.

9. Pour the mixture into an ovenproof dish and sprinkle the top with a little extra grated cheese.

10. Cook under a preheated, moderate broiler, until the top is golden-brown.

Lasagne Rolls

SERVES 4

An interesting way of using sheets of lasagne.

PREPARATION: 10 mins
COOKING: 15 mins

8 lasagne sheets
½ cup button mushrooms, sliced
8 ounces skinned and boned chicken breast
2 tbsps butter or margarine
2 tbsps all-purpose flour
⅔ cup milk
⅔ cup yellow or Swiss cheese, grated
Salt and pepper

1. Fill a large saucepan two-thirds full with salted water. Add a little oil and bring to the boil.

2. Add 1 sheet of lasagne, wait about 2 minutes, then add another sheet. Cook only a few at a time and after about 6-7 minutes remove and rinse under cold water. Allow to drain.

3. Repeat this process until all the lasagne are cooked.

4. Wash and slice the mushrooms; slice the chicken breast into thin strips.

5. Melt half the butter in a small skillet and sauté the mushrooms and the chicken.

6. In a small saucepan, melt the rest of the butter. Stir in the flour and cook one minute.

Step 11 Spread the chicken mixture evenly over each sheet of lasagne and roll up like a jellyroll.

7. Remove the pan from the heat and add the milk gradually, stirring well and returning the pan to the heat between additions, to thicken the sauce.

8. Beat the sauce well and cook 3 minutes.

9. Pour the sauce into the skillet with the chicken and the mushrooms. Add half the cheese and mix well. Season to taste.

10. Lay the sheets of lasagne on a board and divide the chicken mixture equally between them.

11. Spread the chicken mixture evenly over each lasagne sheet and roll up lengthwise, jellyroll fashion.

12. Put the rolls into an ovenproof dish. Sprinkle with the remaining cheese and broil under a pre-heated moderate broiler, until the cheese is bubbly and golden-brown.

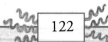

Sunburst Figs make an ideal low calorie dessert.

AMERICA'S BEST

*Low
Calorie*

R E C I P E S

Melon and Prosciutto

SERVES 4

This typically Italian dish makes a light appetizer and is wonderful served on hot summer days.

PREPARATION: 15 mins
115 CALORIES PER SERVING

1 large ripe melon, Cassaba or Crenshaw
16 thin slices prosciutto ham
French flat leaf parsley to garnish

1. Cut the melon in half lengthwise. Using a spoon, scoop out and discard all the seeds and fibers.

Step 1 Using a spoon, scoop out and discard the seeds and fibrous core of the melon.

Note; Prosciutto is raw ham, and is not always available in the U.S. If you cannot get it, use very thinly sliced Smithfield ham.

Step 4 Roll a slice of prosciutto ham around each thin slice of melon.

2. Cut the melon into quarters and carefully peel away the skin using a sharp knife.

3. Cut each quarter into 4 thin slices.

4. Wrap each slice of melon in a slice of the prosciutto ham, and arrange on a serving platter. Chill well and garnish with parsley before serving.

Spicy Tomato Soup

SERVES 4

This highly fragrant and spicy tomato soup makes an interesting low calorie appetizer.

PREPARATION: 15 mins
COOKING: 17-18 mins
41 CALORIES PER SERVING

3 medium tomatoes
1 medium onion, finely chopped
2 tbsps oil
1 green chili pepper, seeded and chopped
3 cloves garlic, crushed
1 tbsp tomato paste
1 quart water, or vegetable broth
4-6 green curry leaves, or ½ tsp curry powder
Salt
Coriander (cilantro) leaves and green
   chilies for garnish

1. Cut a small cross in the skin of each tomato and steep in boiling water 30-40 seconds.

Step 2 Remove the tomatoes from the boiling water and carefully peel away the loosened skin.

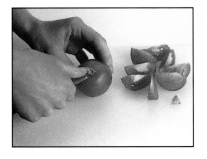

Step 3 Cut away and discard the hard green core from the tomatoes, and chop the flesh roughly with a sharp knife.

2. Remove the tomatoes and carefully peel away the loosened skin with a sharp knife.

3. Remove the core from the tomatoes and roughly chop the flesh.

4. Heat the oil in a large saucepan and gently sauté the onion, chopped chili and garlic for 3-4 minutes until it is soft, but not browned.

5. Stir in the chopped tomatoes and cook 5 minutes, stirring often.

6. Blend the tomato paste with the water and pour this into the onions and tomatoes. Add the curry leaves or powder, season with the salt and simmer 5-7 minutes.

7. Remove the soup from the heat and stir in the coriander leaves and the chili halves.

8. Serve piping hot, discarding the chili garnish before eating.

Carrot Soup

SERVES 4

This warming, tasty soup is filling yet low in calories

PREPARATION: 12 mins
COOKING: 25-30 mins
44 CALORIES PER SERVING

---

1 pound carrots
1 medium onion
1 turnip
2 cloves garlic, crushed
1 quart water or vegetable broth
½ tsp dried thyme
½ tsp ground nutmeg
Salt and pepper, to taste
Toasted sunflower seeds, flaked almonds and
    pistachio nuts, mixed together for garnish

---

1. Peel the carrots and cut them into thick slices.

To chop an onion finely, pierce the peeled onion with a fork and use this to hold the vegetable steady whilst you chop.

Step 6 Purée the soup until it is creamy and smooth.

2. Peel and roughly chop the onion and turnip.

3. Put the vegetables, garlic, and water or broth, into a large saucepan and bring to the boil. Cover the pan, reduce the heat and simmer 20 minutes.

4. Add all the seasonings and simmer a further 5 minutes.

5. Remove the soup from the heat and allow to cool.

6. Using a liquidizer, blend the soup until it is thick and smooth.

7. Reheat the soup, garnishing with the seeds and nuts before serving.

Fresh Tomato Omelet

SERVES 2

Omelets can make substantial low calorie lunches or light meals.

PREPARATION: 25 mins
COOKING: 5 mins
252 CALORIES PER SERVING

1 pound fresh tomatoes
Salt and pepper
4 eggs
4 tbsps water
½ tsp fresh chopped basil
2 tbsps olive or vegetable oil
½ tsp fresh chopped oregano or basil to
  garnish

1. Cut a small cross into the skins of each tomato and plunge them into boiling water. Leave 30 seconds, then remove them with a slotted spoon.

2. Using a sharp knife, carefully peel away the tomato skins and discard them.

Step 3 Remove the seeds and juice from the halved tomatoes with a teaspoon.

Step 5 Whisk the eggs, water and herbs together thoroughly, until they are frothy.

3. Cut the tomatoes in half and remove and discard the seeds, juice, and any tough core.

4. Cut the tomato flesh into thin strips.

5. Break the eggs into a bowl and whisk in the water and chopped herbs. Season with salt and pepper and continue whisking until the egg mixture is frothy.

6. Heat the oil in a large skillet, then pour in the egg mixture.

7. Using a spatula, stir the egg mixture around the pan about 2-3 minutes, or until the eggs are beginning to set.

8. Spread the tomato strips over the partially-cooked eggs, and continue cooking without stirring until the eggs have completely set and the tomatoes are just warmed through.

9. Sprinkle with the additional chopped basi' before serving.

Vegetable Kebobs

SERVES 4

A delicious way to serve fresh vegetables as part of a low calorie diet.

PREPARATION: 30 mins, plus time to marinate
    vegetables
COOKING: 10 mins
83 CALORIES PER SERVING

---

1 large eggplant
Salt
1 large green bell pepper
4 zucchini
12-14 cherry tomatoes
12-14 pearl onions
12-14 button mushrooms
4 tbsps olive oil
2 tbsps lemon juice
½ tsp salt
½ tsp freshly ground black pepper

---

1. Cut the eggplant in half and dice it into 1-inch pieces.

2. Put the eggplant pieces into a large bowl, and sprinkle liberally with salt. Stir well and allow to stand 30 minutes to draw out the bitter juices.

3. Rinse the eggplant pieces thoroughly in a colander under cold water.

4. Cut the bell pepper in half. Remove and discard the core and seeds and cut the pepper

Step 8 Thread the prepared and marinated vegetables alternately onto kebob skewers.

flesh into 1-inch pieces with a sharp knife.

5. Slice the zucchini diagonally into 1-inch pieces.

6. Remove the tough cores from the cherry tomatoes and peel the onions. Rinse the mushrooms under cold water, but do not peel.

7. Put all the prepared vegetables into a large bowl and pour in the remaining ingredients. Mix well to coat evenly, cover and allow to stand about 30 minutes, stirring once or twice.

8. Thread the vegetables alternately onto skewers and arrange them on a broiler pan.

9. Brush the kebobs with the marinade and broil 3-4 minutes, turning frequently and basting with the marinade until they are evenly browned. Serve piping hot.

Ratatouille

SERVES 6

A classic vegetable casserole from the south of France.

PREPARATION: 20 mins, plus 30 mins standing
    time
COOKING: 35 mins
84 CALORIES PER SERVING

2 eggplants
Salt
4 zucchini
4 tbsps olive oil
2 Bermuda (red) onions
2 green or red bell peppers
2 tsps chopped fresh basil
1 large clove garlic, crushed
1 pound 12 ounces canned plum tomatoes
Salt and freshly ground black pepper
⅔ cup dry white wine

1. Cut the eggplants in half lengthwise and score each cut surface diagonally, using the point of a sharp knife.

Step 8 Gently fry the chopped eggplant in the vegetable juices and oil, until they begin to brown.

2. Sprinkle the eggplants liberally with salt and allow to stand 30 minutes. After this time, rinse them thoroughly and pat them dry.

3. Roughly chop the eggplants and slice the zucchini thickly. Set them to one side.

4. Peel the onions and half them. Cut them into thin slices with a sharp knife.

5. Cut the bell peppers in half lengthwise and remove and discard the seeds and white parts. Chop the flesh roughly.

6. Heat the oil in a large saucepan, and sauté the onion slices for 5 minutes until they are soft.

7. Stir in the peppers and zucchini, and cook gently 5 minutes until they begin to soften. Remove all the vegetables from the pan and set aside.

8. Put the chopped eggplants into the saucepan with the vegetable juices. Cook gently until the mixture begins to brown, then add all the other ingredients to the pan.

9. Add the canned tomatoes, garlic, and basil to the saucepan along with the sautéed vegetables, mixing well. Bring to the boil, then reduce the heat and simmer 15 minutes.

10. Add the wine to the pan and continue cooking for a further 15 minutes before serving.

Casserole of Veal and Mushrooms

SERVES 6

Veal is a low-fat meat and is delicious when served in this tomato and mushroom sauce.

PREPARATION: 30 mins
COOKING: 1hr 30 mins
275 CALORIES PER SERVING

3 pounds lean veal
Salt and pepper
4 tbsps olive oil
2 shallots, finely chopped
½ clove garlic, peeled and crushed
6 tbsps dry white wine
1¼ cups strong beef broth or consommé
1 cup canned tomatoes, drained and chopped
1 bouquet garni (parsley, bayleaf, chervil and thyme)
2 strips lemon peel
½ cup button mushrooms
2 tbsps fresh chopped parsley

1. Dice the meat into bite-size pieces, using a sharp knife.

2. Sprinkle the pieces of meat with salt and pepper, then allow to stand about 30 minutes.

3. Heat half of the oil in a large skillet, and sauté the pieces of meat 5-10 minutes, stirring frequently. Remove the meat from the pan and set it aside.

4. Add the shallots and garlic to the oil and

Step 4 Cook the garlic and shallots in the hot oil and meat juices gently, taking care to soften but not brown them.

meat juices in the pan, lower the heat and cook until softened. Return the veal to the pan and mix well.

5. Add the wine, broth, tomatoes, bouquet garni, and lemon peel to the meat mixture, and bring to the boil.

6. Transfer the veal to an ovenproof casserole. Cover with a tight-fitting lid and bake in a pre-heated 325°F oven about 1¼ hours, or until the meat is tender.

7. Heat the remaining oil in a clean skillet, and cook the mushrooms 2-3 minutes.

8. When the meat in the casserole is tender, stir in the mushrooms and continue cooking in the oven a further 15 minutes.

9. Sprinkle with the chopped parsley before serving.

Chicken Escalopes

SERVES 4

*Although the chicken is sautéed in oil, it is only enough to brown the
meat without adding too many calories.*

PREPARATION: 20 mins
COOKING: 10-15 mins
300 CALORIES PER SERVING

4 chicken breasts, boned and skinned
1 egg white
8 tbsps wholewheat breadcrumbs
1 tbsp chopped fresh sage
Salt and pepper
2 tbsps walnut oil
½ cup low-calorie mayonnaise
⅔ cup plain yogurt
1 tsp grated fresh horseradish
2 tbsps chopped walnuts
Lemon slices and chopped walnuts to garnish

1. Pat the chicken breasts dry with kitchen paper.

2. Whisk the egg whites with a fork until they just begin to froth, but are still liquid.

3. Carefully brush all surfaces of the chicken breasts with the beaten egg white.

4. Put the breadcrumbs onto a shallow plate and stir in the chopped sage. Season with a little salt and pepper.

5. Place the chicken breasts, one at a time, onto the plate of breadcrumbs and sage, and

Step 5 Press the bread-crumb-and-sage mixture onto the chicken breasts.

carefully press this mixture onto the surfaces of the chicken.

6. Put the oil into a large shallow skillet, and gently sauté the chicken 5 minutes on each side. Test that the meat is cooked by piercing with a skewer. If the juices do not run clear, sautée a few minutes more. Set aside, and keep warm.

7. Mix all the remaining ingredients except for the garnish in a small bowl, whisking well to blend the yogurt and mayonnaise evenly.

8. Place the cooked chicken breasts on a serving platter, and spoon a little of the sauce over. Serve garnished with the lemon slices and additional chopped nuts.

Paprika Schnitzel

SERVES 4

Peppers, paprika, and wine give a hearty flavor to this easily-prepared dish.

PREPARATION: 30 mins
COOKING: approximately 20 mins
230 CALORIES PER SERVING

8 thin slices pork fillet, sliced lengthwise
Salt and pepper
1 garlic clove, crushed
3 tbsps vegetable oil
1 medium onion
1 red bell pepper
1 green bell pepper
1 tbsp paprika
⅔ cup beef broth
½ cup red wine
3 tbsps tomato paste
⅔ cup plain low fat yogurt

1. Trim the slices of pork to remove any fat, and flatten them out with a rolling pin until they are ¼-inch thick.

2. Rub both sides of the pork fillets with salt, pepper, and garlic, then allow to stand in a refrigerator for 30 minutes.

3. Heat the oil in a large skillet, and cook the pork fillets until they are well browned and cooked right through, approximately 4 minutes on each side.

4. Remove the pork from the pan, set aside, and keep warm.

Step 1 Flatten the pork fillets out with a rolling pin until they are ¼-inch thick.

5. Peel the onion and thinly slice it into rings. Cut the peppers in half and remove and discard the seeds and white parts. Slice the peppers lengthwise into thin strips.

6. Add the onion rings and the sliced peppers to the oil and meat juices in the skillet, and cook quickly about 3-4 minutes until they are soft.

7. Add the paprika, broth, wine, and tomato paste to the skillet and bring the mixture to the boil.

8. Reduce the heat and simmer until the liquid has evaporated and the sauce has thickened. Season to taste.

9. Arrange the pork slices on a serving platter, and pour the paprika sauce over the top of them.

10. Beat the yogurt in a bowl until it is smooth, then carefully drizzle it over the paprika sauce to make an attractive pattern. Serve hot.

Kidneys with Mustard Sauce

SERVES 4

Lambs' kidneys have a delicate flavor, which a mustard sauce complements perfectly.

PREPARATION: 25 mins
COOKING: 15 mins
220 CALORIES PER SERVING

---

4 tbsps vegetable oil
1½ pounds lambs' kidneys
1-2 shallots, peeled and finely chopped
1¼ cups dry white wine
3 tbsps Dijon-style mustard
Salt, pepper and lemon juice, to taste
2 tbsps fresh chopped parsley

---

1. Cut the kidneys in half lengthwise, and carefully snip out the core and tough tubes.

2. Heat the oil in a large skillet, and gently sauté the kidneys about 10 minutes, stirring them frequently until they are light brown on all sides. Remove the kidneys from the pan and keep them warm.

Step 1 Trim any fat or tubes away from the core of each kidney, using a sharp knife or small pair of scissors.

Step 2 Sauté the kidneys in the hot oil, stirring them frequently to brown evenly on all sides.

3. Add the shallots to the pan and cook about 1 minute, stirring frequently until they soften.

4. Add the wine and bring to the boil, stirring constantly and scraping the pan to remove any brown juices.

5. Allow the wine to boil rapidly 3-4 minutes, until it has reduced by about half. Remove the pan from the heat.

6. Using a balloon whisk or fork, mix the mustard into the reduced wine along with salt, pepper, lemon juice to taste, and half of the fresh chopped parsley.

7. Return the kidneys to the pan and cook over a low heat 1-2 minutes, stirring all the time to heat the kidneys through evenly. Serve immediately, sprinkled with the remaining parsley.

Broiled Whole Fish

SERVES 4

Broiling fish with herbs and lemon is a delicious, healthy way to cook fish.

PREPARATION: 20 mins
COOKING: 16-20 mins, depending upon the size of the fish
APPROX. 180 CALORIES PER SERVING

---

2 large bream, porgy or other whole fish
Fresh thyme and oregano
Olive oil
Lemon juice
Salt and pepper
Lemon wedges

Step 1 To make lemon wedges cut the ends off the lemons, then cut in 4 or 8 wedges.

1. Preheat a broiler. Gut the fish and rinse it well. Pat dry and sprinkle the cavity with salt, pepper, and lemon juice. Place sprigs of herbs inside.

2. Make 3 diagonal cuts on the sides of the fish with a sharp knife. Place the fish on the broiler rack and sprinkle with olive oil and lemon juice.

3. Cook on both sides until golden brown and crisp. This should take about 8-10 minutes per side, depending on the thickness of the fish.

4. Serve the fish on a large platter surrounded with lemon wedges.

Step 2 Use a sharp knife to make diagonal cuts on both sides of each fish.

Sole Kebobs

SERVES 4

Fish is highly nutritious, easy to cook, and makes an ideal contribution to a healthy diet.

PREPARATION: 30 mins, plus marinating time
COOKING: 8 mins
254 CALORIES PER SERVING

8 fillets of sole
4 tbsps olive oil
1 clove garlic, peeled and crushed
Juice ½ lemon
Finely grated rind ½ lemon
Salt and pepper
3 drops of Tabasco sauce
3 zucchini
1 green bell pepper
Freshly chopped parsley for garnish

1. Using a sharp knife, carefully peel the skin from the backs of each sole fillet.

2. Cut each sole fillet in half lengthwise, and roll each slice up like a jellyroll.

3. Mix together the oil, garlic, lemon juice,

Step 1 Use a sharp knife to cut between the meat of the fish and the skin. Lift the meat up and away as you cut.

Step 7 Thread the marinated rolls of fish onto kebob skewers, alternating these with vegetables.

rind, and seasonings in a small bowl.

4. Put the rolls of fish into a shallow dish and pour over the marinade. Cover and allow to stand in a cool place for at least 2 hours.

5. Cut the zucchini into ¼-inch slices.

6. Cut the peppers in half lengthwise and remove the white core and the seeds. Chop the pepper flesh into 1-inch squares.

7. Carefully thread the marinated sole fillets onto kebob skewers, alternating these with pieces of the prepared vegetables. Brush each kebob with a little of the marinade.

8. Arrange the kebobs on a broiler pan and cook under a moderately hot broiler for about 8 minutes, turning frequently, and brushing with the extra marinade to keep them moist.

9. Arrange the kebobs on a serving platter, and sprinkle with the chopped parsley.

Watercress and Orange Salad

SERVES 4-6

This colorful salad looks best when served on a bed of grated carrot.

PREPARATION: 20 mins
200 CALORIES PER SERVING

---

3 large bunches of watercress
4 oranges
6 tbsps oil
Juice and rind of 1 orange
Pinch sugar
1 tsp lemon juice
Salt and pepper

---

1. Wash the watercress and carefully cut away any thick stalks. Break the watercress into small sprigs, discarding any yellow leaves.

Step 2 Carefully peel the oranges using a sharp knife, and collecting any juices in a small bowl.

Step 3 Cut the orange segments carefully from between the inner membranes using a sharp knife.

2. Carefully remove the peel and white parts from the oranges using a sharp knife. Catch any juice that spills in a small bowl.

3. Cut carefully, remove the fleshy segments from between the thin membrane inside the orange.

4. Arrange the watercress with the orange segments on a serving platter.

5. Put the remaining ingredients into the bowl with the reserved orange juice, and mix together well.

6. Pour the salad dressing over the oranges and watercress just before serving, to prevent the watercress from going limp.

Tuna, Bean and Tomato Salad

SERVES 6

This salad is a meal in itself, containing a good balance of protein and fiber.

PREPARATION: 25 mins, plus overnight soaking
180 CALORIES PER SERVING

---

1 cup dried flageolet beans
¾ canned tuna in brine
Juice of 1 lemon
½ cup olive oil
1 tsp chopped parsley, basil or marjoram
Salt and pepper
8 firm tomatoes

---

1. Put the beans into a bowl and pour over enough cold water to just cover. Allow to soak overnight.

2. Drain the beans and put them into a saucepan. Cover with boiling water, then simmer at least 1 hour. Drain thoroughly and cool.

3. Drain the can of tuna and flake it into a bowl.

Step 5 Mix the dressing into the salad by tossing it carefully, to ensure that the tuna does not break up too much.

Step 8 When blanched, the skins on the tomatoes should peel away very easily if you use a sharp knife.

4. Put the lemon juice, olive oil, herbs, and seasoning into a small bowl and whisk together with a fork.

5. Stir the beans into the tuna fish and mix in the dressing, tossing the salad together carefully so that the dressing is thoroughly incorporated.

6. Adjust the seasoning and arrange the salad in a mound on a shallow serving platter.

7. Cut a small cross into the skins of the tomato and plunge them into boiling water for 30 seconds.

8. Using a sharp knife, carefully peel away the skins from the tomatoes.

9. Slice the tomatoes thinly and arrange them around the edge of the bean and tuna salad. Serve immediately.

Frozen Lime and Blueberry Cream – an
impressive finale to a special meal.

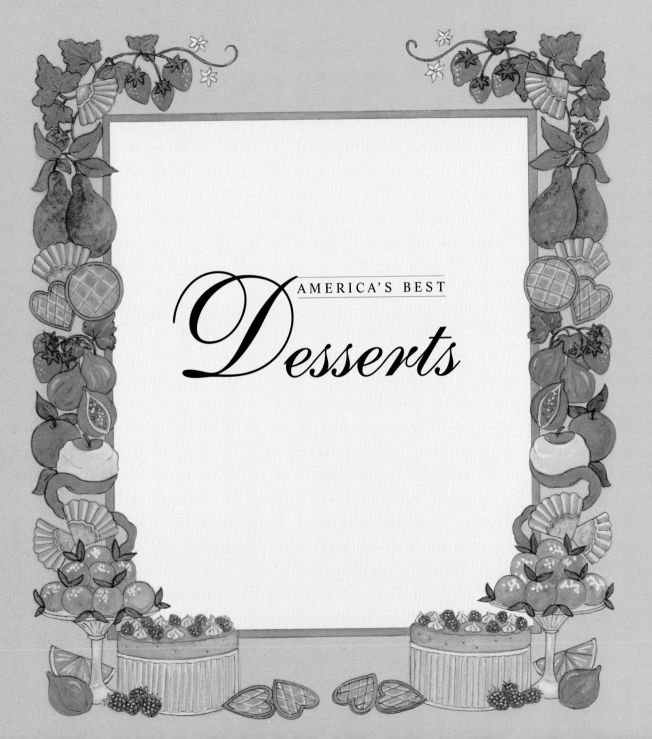

AMERICA'S BEST

Desserts

Parfait Au Cassis

SERVES 4

A rich and creamy dessert with a delicious fruity tang.

PREPARATION: 30 mins, plus freezing
COOKING: 30 mins

---

3 cups blueberries
2 tbsps blackcurrant liqueur
3 egg yolks
½ cup light brown sugar
1½ cups single cream
1½ cups whipped cream
Blueberries and mint leaves, to decorate

---

1. Purée the blueberries in a liquidizer or food processor, and push through a sieve with a wooden spoon to remove the skin and pips. Add the cassis to the purée and freeze until it becomes slushy, stirring occasionally to prevent large ice crystals from forming.

2. Whisk the egg yolks and sugar together until they become very thick and foaming. Heat

Step 2 Whisk the egg yolks and sugar together until they become thick and foaming.

Step 3 Cool the mixture quickly by standing the bowl in iced water.

the single cream in a small pan until almost, but not quite, boiling. Gradually add the cream to the egg mixture, stirring constantly.

3. Place the bowl over a pan of gently simmering water and cook, stirring constantly, until the mixture thickens. Cool quickly by standing the bowl in ice water, then fold in the whipped cream.

4. Freeze until the mixture is almost solid, then beat with an electric mixer or in a food processor until slushy. Break up the blueberry mixture with a fork or electric whisk and fold into the cream mixture to give a marbled effect. Divide the mixture between 6 freezer-proof dessert glasses and freeze until required.

5. Refrigerate 30 minutes before serving, and decorate with blueberries and mint leaves.

Apple Nut Tart

SERVES 6

The sweet, spicy flavor of cinnamon blends perfectly with the apples and nuts in this traditional dessert.

PREPARATION: 20 mins
COOKING: 40 mins

2 cups all-purpose flour
⅔ cup superfine sugar
½ cup butter, cut into pieces
1 egg
4 cups dessert apples, peeled, cored and sliced
½ cup hazelnuts, coarsely ground
1 tsp ground cinnamon
Juice of 1 lemon
3 tbsps apricot brandy (optional)
½ cup warmed apricot jam
2 tbsps chopped hazelnuts

1. Sieve together the flour and ½ cup of the sugar into a bowl. Rub in the butter until the mixture resembles fine breadcrumbs.

Step 4 Layer the apples and ground hazelnuts in the pastry case.

Step 5 Pour the melted jam over the layers of apples and hazelnuts.

2. Make a well in the center of the flour mixture and drop in the egg. Gradually incorporate the flour into the egg using a knife or, as the mixture becomes firmer, your fingers. Continue kneading the mixture together, until it forms a smooth dough.

3. Wrap the dough in plastic wrap and chill at least 30 minutes, then roll out and use to line an 8-inch greased pie pan.

4. Layer the apple slices and the ground hazelnuts in the pastry case. Sprinkle with the cinnamon, remaining sugar, lemon juice, and apricot brandy, if using.

5. Pour the warmed jam over the apple mixture, and sprinkle with the chopped hazelnuts. Bake in a preheated oven at 425°F, for 35-40 minutes or until the fruit is soft and the tart is golden-brown.

Mocha Ice Cream Pie

MAKES 1 PIE

Unbelievably simple, yet incredibly delicious and impressive, this is a perfect ending to a summer meal.

PREPARATION: 25 mins, plus freezing

12 Oreo cookies
6 tbsps melted butter or margarine
1 cup flaked coconut
2 squares plain chocolate, melted
2 quarts coffee-flavored ice cream

1. Crush the cookies with a rolling pin or in a food processor. Mix with melted butter or margarine.

2. Press into an 8½-inch springform pan. Chill thoroughly in the refrigerator.

3. Meanwhile, combine 4 tbsps of the coconut with the melted chocolate. When cooled but not solidified, add about 1 pint of the coffee ice cream, mixing well.

Step 2 Press the crust mixture into the base of a springform pan.

Step 5 Spread the coffee ice cream carefully over the chocolate-coconut layer and re-freeze.

4. Spread the mixture on top of the crust and freeze until firm.

5. Soften the remaining ice cream with an electric mixer or food processor, and spread over the chocolate-coconut layer. Re-freeze until firm.

6. Toast the remaining coconut under a moderate broiler, stirring frequently until pale golden-brown. Allow to cool completely.

7. Remove the pie from the freezer and leave in the refrigerator 30 minutes before serving. Push up the base of the pan and place the pie on a serving platter. Sprinkle with the toasted coconut. Cut into wedges to serve.

Zuppa Inglese

SERVES 6-8

The Italian name means English soup, but this is a rich, thick, creamy dessert.

PREPARATION: 25 mins plus chilling

2 tbsps cornstarch
2½ cups milk
2 eggs, lightly beaten
2 tbsps sugar
Grated rind of ½ lemon
Pinch nutmeg
4 cups ripe strawberries
16 finger cookies
Amaretto liqueur
⅔ cup whipping cream

1. Mix the cornstarch with some of the milk. Beat the eggs, sugar, lemon rind, and nutmeg together and add the remaining milk. Mix with the cornstarch mixture in a heavy-based pan and stir over a gentle heat until the mixture thickens and comes to the boil.

Step 1 Combine the custard ingredients and cook until the mixture thickens and coats the back of a spoon.

Step 3 Place a layer of finger cookies and strawberries in a serving dish and coat with a layer of custard. Repeat with remaining ingredients.

2. Allow to boil 1 minute or until the mixture coats the back of a spoon. Place a sheet of parchment paper directly on top of the custard and allow it to cool slightly.

3. Save 8 even-sized strawberries for decoration and hull the remaining ones. Place half of the finger cookies in the bottom of a glass bowl and sprinkle with some amaretto. Cut the strawberries in half and place a layer on top of the finger cookies. Pour a layer of custard on top and repeat with the remaining cookies and sliced strawberries. Top with another layer of custard and allow to cool completely.

4. Whip the cream and spread a thin layer over the top of the set custard. Pipe the remaining cream around the edge of the dish and decorate with the reserved strawberries. Serve chilled.

Raspberry Soufflé

SERVES 6

This light dessert is the perfect finale for a dinner party.

PREPARATION: 40 mins, plus chilling

4 cups raspberries
3 tbsps superfine sugar
1 tbsp unflavored gelatin
⅔ cup hot water
4 eggs, separated
1¼ cups heavy cream

1. Prepare a 6-inch soufflé dish by tightly tying a lightly oiled sheet of parchment paper carefully around the outside edge of the soufflé dish, allowing it to stand approximately 4 inches above the rim of the dish.

2. Reserve a few of the raspberries for decoration, and purée the remainder with the sugar in a liquidizer or food processor.

3. Rub the puréed raspberries through a nylon sieve to remove the seeds.

4. Dissolve the gelatin in the hot water, stirring gently until it is completely dissolved, and the liquid is clear.

5. Allow the gelatin to cool slightly and then beat it into the raspberry purée along with the egg yolks, mixing until all ingredients are well blended. Chill until partially set.

Step 1 Tie a sheet of parchment paper around the soufflé dish, to form a collar rising above the rim of the dish.

6. Whisk the egg whites until they form soft peaks.

7. Lightly whip half of the heavy cream into soft peaks.

8. Remove the partially-set raspberry mixture from the refrigerator, and carefully fold in the cream and the egg whites, using a metal tablespoon, blending lightly but thoroughly until the mixture is smooth.

9. Turn the mixture into the prepared dish – it should rise about 1 inch above the rim of the dish inside the paper collar. Allow to set in the refrigerator.

10. When completely set, carefully remove the collar, and decorate the soufflé with the remaining whipped cream and the reserved raspberries.

Coffee Pecan Pie

SERVES 6-8

This traditional American pie is ideal for serving after a celebration meal.

PREPARATION: 20 mins, plus chilling

1 cup crushed graham crackers
2 tbsps melted butter
1 cup pecan halves
1 cup marshmallows
1¼ cups strong black coffee
1 tbsp unflavored gelatin
3 tbsps hot water
1 egg white
⅔ cup light whipped soft cheese

1. Mix together the cracker crumbs and the melted butter. Press onto the base and halfway up the sides of a well-greased 7-inch springform pan and chill at least 1 hour.

2. Reserve 8 pecan halves for decoration, and chop the remainder finely.

3. In a large saucepan, dissolve the marshmallows in the coffee by heating gently

Step 2 Chop the remainder of the pecans.

Step 3 Put the marshmallows and the coffee into a large saucepan, and heat gently, stirring until the marsh-mallows have dissolved.

and stirring frequently.

4. Sprinkle the gelatin onto the hot water and stir until it is clear and has dissolved.

5. Carefully pour the gelatin into the marsh-mallow mixture, and stir well to ensure that it is evenly mixed in. Leave the marshmallow mixture to cool until it is almost set.

6. Whisk the egg white until it forms soft peaks, fold this into the whipped soft cheese, and then fold this into the marshmallow mixture, using a metal spoon to incorporate as much air as possible. Make sure all is evenly blended.

7. Stir in the chopped nuts and pour the mixture onto the chilled cracker base. Chill the pie at least 3 hours until completely set.

8. Remove the sides of the pan and slide the pie carefully onto a serving dish. Decorate with the reserved nut halves.

Chocolate Almond Stuffed Figs

SERVES 4

A positively luxurious dessert that is deceptively easy to prepare.

PREPARATION: 20 mins
COOKING: 25 mins

---

4 ripe figs
2 tbsps liquid honey
1 square semi-sweet baking chocolate
6 tbsps ground almonds

Cinnamon sauce
1¼ cups single cream
1 stick cinnamon
2 egg yolks
4 tbsps sugar
Ground cinnamon and blanched almond
    halves, to garnish

---

1. Make a cross-cut in each fig without cutting right down through the base. Carefully press the 4 sections of the fig out so that it looks like a flower.

2. Melt the honey and chocolate in a bowl over a pan of hot water.

3. Set aside to cool slightly and then mix in the ground almonds.

4. When the mixture has cooled completely, spoon an equal amount into the center of each fig.

Step 7
Combine cream and eggs and cook over gentle heat until mixture coats the back of a spoon.

5. Meanwhile, prepare the sauce; pour the cream into a deep saucepan and add the cinnamon stick. Bring to just under the boil, remove from the heat, and leave to infuse.

6. Beat the egg yolks and the sugar together until pale and thick, then gradually strain the infused cream over the mixture.

7. Return the mixture to the saucepan and stir over a gentle heat until it just coats the back of a spoon. Leave to cool until just warm.

8. To serve, pour a little of the cream onto each serving plate and tilt the plate slowly to coat the base. Place a filled fig on top of each and sprinkle around some of the ground cinnamon, topping each fig with a blanched almond.

Weinschaum

SERVES 4-6

This is a light and luscious dessert that can also be a sauce. Its name means
"wine foam," which describes it perfectly.

PREPARATION: 15 mins, plus chilling

2¼ cups dry white wine
⅔ cup water
4 eggs
½ cup sugar
Orange zest or crystallized rose or violet petals,
    for decoration

---

1. Place the wine and water in the top of a double boiler over boiling water. Make sure the top half of the double boiler does not actually

Step 2 Check the base of the bowl or double boiler. If very hot, place in a bowl of ice water and continue whisking.

Step 2 When thick enough, lift beaters or whisk and draw a trail of mixture across the bowl. The trail should hold its shape.

touch the boiling water. Add the eggs and sugar and beat the ingredients vigorously with a wire whisk or an electric mixer.

2. When the custard thickens, it should hold a ribbon trail when the whisk or the beaters are lifted. Do not allow the custard to boil.

3. Spoon into serving dishes and decorate with strips of orange zest or crystallized flower petals. Serve hot or chill thoroughly before serving.

170

Frozen Lime and Blueberry Cream

SERVES 6

An impressive dessert that's perfect for entertaining.

PREPARATION: 40 mins, plus overnight freezing

Juice and zested rind of 4 limes
1 cup sugar
1 cup blueberries
3 egg whites
1¼ cups whipped cream

1. Measure the lime juice and make up to ⅓ cup with water if necessary.

2. Combine with the sugar in a heavy-based pan and bring to the boil slowly to dissolve the sugar.

3. When the mixture forms a clear sirup, boil rapidly to 248°F on a candy thermometer.

4. Meanwhile, combine the blueberries with about 4 tbsps water in a small saucepan. Bring

Step 6 Fold the cream and the fruit purée into the egg whites, marbling the purée through the mixture.

to the boil and then simmer, covered, until very soft. Purée, then sieve to remove the seeds and skin, and set aside to cool.

5. Whisk the egg whites until soft but not dry and then pour on the hot sugar sirup in a steady stream, whisking constantly. Add the lime rind and allow the meringue to cool.

6. When cold, fold in the whipped cream. Add the purée and marble through the mixture with a spatula. Do not over-fold. Pour the mixture into a lightly-oiled mold or bowl and freeze until firm.

7. Leave in the refrigerator 30 minutes before serving or dip the mold in hot water for about 10 seconds. Place a plate over the bottom of the mold, invert and shake to unmold. Garnish with extra whipped cream and lime slices.

Step 5 Pour the sirup gradually onto the whisked egg whites, beating constantly.

Tarte Tatin

SERVES 6-8

This classic French dessert is one of the tastiest ways of serving apples.

PREPARATION: 40 mins, plus chilling
COOKING: 20-25 mins

Pastry
2 cups all-purpose flour
1 stick butter, diced
1 egg yolk
2 tsps superfine sugar
½ tsp salt
2 tsps water

Filling
6 tbsps butter
6 tbsps superfine sugar
4 large tart apples, peeled, cored and quartered

---

1. To make the dough, sift the flour onto a work surface. Make a well in the center and add the remaining dough ingredients to the well, mixing them together with your fingertips.

2. Gradually draw in the flour, until the

Step 5 Neatly pack the apples into the skillet.

Step 6
Carefully lay the dough over the apples, tucking the edges down inside the pan.

mixture forms coarse crumbs. Add a little extra water if necessary.

3. Draw the mixture into a ball, then knead 1-2 minutes on a lightly-floured surface until smooth. Cover and chill 30 minutes.

4. Melt the butter in a 10-inch flameproof and ovenproof skillet, or tarte tatin pan.

5. Add the sugar and neatly pack in the apples. Cook 15-20 minutes, until the sugar caramelizes. Then allow to cool slightly.

6. Roll the pastry out to a circle slightly larger than the pan. Place it over the apples, tucking the edges down inside the pan.

7. Bake in an oven preheated to 425°F 20-25 minutes or until the pastry is crisp and golden.

8. Allow to cool in the pan 10 minutes, then turn out onto a serving platter and serve immediately with heavy cream.

Caramel Oranges

SERVES 4

This is one of the classic Italian desserts.

PREPARATION: 25 mins, plus chilling
COOKING: 25 mins

---

4 large oranges
1¾ cups sugar
1¾ cups water
2 tbsps brandy or orange liqueur

---

1. Use a vegetable peeler to remove the rind from two of the oranges. Take off any white parts and slice the rind into very thin julienne strips with a sharp knife.

2. Place the julienne strips in a small saucepan, cover with water and bring to the boil. Drain, then dry.

3. Cut the ends off all the oranges, then take the peel and white part off in very thin strips, using a sawing motion. Cut the oranges horizontally into slices about ¼-inch thick.

Step 1 Peel the oranges in thin strips with a vegetable peeler. Remove any white parts and cut into thin julienne strips.

Step 3 Use a serrated knife to take off orange peel in thin strips.

4. Stir the sugar and 1½ cups of the water in a heavy-based pan over medium heat until the sugar has dissolved. Add the drained orange peel strips to the pan.

5. Boil the syrup gently, uncovered, about 10 minutes or until the orange strips are glazed. Remove the strips from the pan and place on a lightly-oiled plate.

6. Return the pan to a high heat and boil, uncovered, until it turns a pale golden-brown. Remove from the heat immediately and quickly add the remaining water. Return to a gentle heat for a few minutes to dissolve the hardened caramel, then allow to cool completely. Stir in the brandy.

7. Arrange the orange slices in a serving dish, and pour the cooled syrup over them. Pile the glazed orange strips on top and refrigerate for several hours, or overnight, before serving.

Fresh Fruit in Tulip Cups

SERVES 4

Elegant presentation is what gives this simple fruit dessert its special, dinner-party touch.

PREPARATION: 10 mins, plus 1 hr standing
COOKING: 8-10 mins

Tulip cups
1 egg white
4 tbsps sugar
2 tbsps all-purpose flour
2 tbsps melted butter
2 tbsps ground almonds
1 tbsp flaked almonds

Fruit filling
1 mango
2 figs
10 strawberries
1 kiwi
10 cherries
Vanilla ice cream
1 tbsp flaked almonds

1. To make the tulip cups, mix the egg white with the sugar, then add the flour, melted butter, and the ground almonds, beating well to incorporate all the ingredients. Set aside to rest for 1 hour.

2. Peel the fruit as necessary and cut into attractive shapes.

3. Place 1 tbsp of the mixture on a nonstick

Step 5 While the cookies are still hot, mold them by pressing them into small bowls so they have crinkled edges.

baking tray, and spread it out well using the back of a spoon. Repeat three times. Sprinkle the flaked almonds over the mixture, dividing them equally between the four rounds.

4. Bake in an oven preheated to 400°F 8-10 minutes or until lightly brown.

5. When cooked, and while they are still hot, mold the cookies by pressing them into individual brioche pans or small bowls. Allow them to cool and harden in the molds.

6. When cool, remove the tulip cups from their molds and place on serving plates. Fill with the fruit, top with a little vanilla ice cream, and decorate with the remaining 1 tbsp flaked almonds.

Apricot Fool

SERVES 4

This dish makes a very quick and easy dessert.

PREPARATION: 10 mins, plus soaking
COOKING: 30 mins

---

1 cup dried apricots
1 ripe banana
1 cup thick-set plain yogurt
1 egg, separated
Chocolate curls or toasted, slivered almonds

---

1. Soak the apricots in water for at least 1 hour. Simmer in the water 20-30 minutes or until tender, then remove with a slotted spoon to a blender or food processor, and purée until smooth.

2. Mash the banana and add to the apricot purée.

3. Fold the yogurt into the fruit mixture along with the egg yolk.

4. Whisk the egg white until stiff, then gently fold into the fruit mixture. Spoon into individual dessert glasses and chill. Decorate with curls of chocolate or toasted almonds.

Poires au Vin Rouge

SERVES 6

A great way of using firm cooking pears to their best advantage.
They look beautiful served in a glass bowl.

PREPARATION: 25 mins
COOKING: 20 mins

2½ cups dry red wine
Juice of ½ lemon
1 strip lemon peel
1 cup sugar
1 small piece stick cinnamon
6 small ripe but firm pears, peeled, but with the
 stalks left on
1 tsp cornstarch (optional)
4 tbsps toasted flaked almonds (optional)
½ cup whipped cream (optional)

---

1. Bring the wine, lemon juice and peel, sugar, and cinnamon to the boil in a deep saucepan or flameproof casserole in which the pears fit snugly. Stir until the sugar dissolves and then allow to boil rapidly 1 minute.

Step 2 Peel the pears length-wise and remove the eye from the bottom.

Step 2 Place the pears in the simmering wine, upright or on their sides.

2. Peel the pears lengthwise and remove the small eye from the bottom of each. Place upright in the simmering wine. Allow to cook slowly 20 minutes, or until soft but not mushy. If the syrup does not completely cover the pears, allow to cook on their sides and turn and baste them frequently. Cool the in the syrup until lukewarm and then remove them. Remove the cinnamon stick and the lemon peel and discard.

3. If the syrup is still very thin, remove pears, boil to reduce slightly or mix 1 tbsp cornstarch with a little cold water, add some of the warm syrup and return the cornstarch to the rest of the syrup. Bring to the boil, stirring constantly, until thickened and clear. Spoon the syrup over the pears and refrigerate or serve warm. Decorate with toasted flaked almonds and serve with lightly-whipped cream if wished.

Vanilla Cream Melba

SERVES 4

Pasta is wonderful in desserts as it soaks up flavors beautifully.

PREPARATION: 15 mins, plus chilling
COOKING: 10 mins

3 ounces small pasta shells
2 cups milk
3 tbsps brown sugar
Few drops vanilla extract
⅔ cup lightly whipped cream
1 large can peach halves
1 tsp cinnamon (optional)

Melba sauce
2 cups raspberries
2 tbsps confectioner's sugar

Step 4 Serve the pasta with peach halves.

1. Cook the pasta in the milk and sugar until tender. Stir regularly, being careful not to allow it to boil over.

2. Draw off the heat and stir in vanilla extract. Pour the pasta into a bowl and allow to cool. When cool, fold in the cream and leave to chill in the refrigerator.

3. Meanwhile, make the Melba sauce. Purée the raspberries in a blender or food processor, then push the purée through a fine nylon sieve. Mix in some confectioner's sugar to taste.

4. Serve the vanilla cream in shallow dishes. Set the peach halves on top and pour the Melba sauce over them. Dust with cinnamon if wished.

Step 2 Fold cream into cooled pasta mixture.

Lemon and Ginger Cheesecake

SERVES 6-8

This fresh, creamy-tasting cheesecake is full of wholesome ingredients.

PREPARATION: 30 mins, plus chilling

3 tbsps butter, melted
2 tbsps soft brown sugar
1 cup crushed wholewheat cookies
1 cup soft cheese
2 eggs, separated
Finely grated rind 1 lemon
2 tbsps soft brown sugar
⅔ cup plain yogurt
1 tbsp unflavored gelatin
3 tbsps hot water
Juice ½ lemon
3 pieces preserved stem ginger, rinsed in warm
  water, and chopped
4 tbsps thick plain yogurt

1. Mix the melted butter with the sugar and crushed cookies. Press the mixture evenly over the base of a greased 7-inch loose-bottomed

Step 1 Spread the cookie crumb mixture evenly over the base of the pie pan, drawing it slightly up the sides of the pan.

Step 4 Thoroughly mix in the dissolved gelatin, along with the lemon juice. Stir the mixture well, to ensure that the gelatin is evenly blended.

pie pan and chill for at least 1 hour.

2. Beat the soft cheese with the egg yolks, lemon rind, and sugar. Stir in the yogurt.

3. Dissolve the gelatin in the water, and add this to the cheese mixture, stirring thoroughly, to incorporate evenly.

4. Stir in the lemon juice, and put the cheese mixture to one side until it is on the point of setting.

5. Whisk the egg whites until they are stiff but not dry, and fold them lightly, but thoroughly, into the cheese mixture, together with the chopped ginger. Spoon into the prepared pie pan, smoothing the surface.

6. Chill the cheesecake 3-4 hours, until the filling has set completely. Swirl the natural yogurt over the top and decorate with matchstick strips of lemon zest, or lemon twists.

My Favorite Recipes

My Favorite Recipes

Notes

_____

_____

_____

_____

_____

_____

_____

_____

_____

_____

_____

_____

_____

_____

Index